M000197756

AS A LITTLE CHILD

André Ravier, SJ

As a Little Child

The Mysticism of "Little Children,"
and of "Those Who are Like Them"

Translated by
Cornelius Michael Buckley, SJ

ALBA·HOUSE   NEW·YORK

SOCIETY OF ST. PAUL, 2187 VICTORY BLVD., STATEN ISLAND, NEW YORK 10314

ST PAULS

Originally published in French by Librairie Arthème Fayard
in the *Collection Lumière, Série Lumière Vérité*, 1992
under the title *Comme un enfant: Mystique pour tous*

Library of Congress Cataloging-in-Publication Data

Ravier, André.
    [Comme un enfant. English]
    As a little child: the mysticism of little children and of those who
    are like them / André Ravier; translated by Cornelius Michael
    Buckley.
        p.   cm.
    ISBN 0-8189-0796-7
        1. Bible. N.T. — Meditations. 2. Spiritual life — Catholic Church.
    3. Catholic Church — doctrines. I. Title.
    BS2341.3.R3813   1998
    242'.5 — dc21   97-19566
                                                                   CIP

Nihil Obstat: *Imprimatur:*
Paris, October 31, 1991   Beauvais, November 20, 1991
Jacques Orgebin, SJ   Adolphe-Marie Hardy
Provincial of France   Bishop of Beauvais

The Nihil Obstat and Imprimatur are official declarations that a book or
pamphlet is free of doctrinal or moral error. No implication is contained
therein that those who have granted the Nihil Obstat and Imprimatur
agree with the contents, opinions or statements expressed.

Produced and designed in the United States of America by the
Fathers and Brothers of the Society of St. Paul,
2187 Victory Boulevard, Staten Island, New York 10314,
as part of their communications apostolate.

ISBN: 0-8189-0796-7

Printing Information:

Current Printing - first digit   1   2   3   4   5   6   7   8   9   10

Year of Current Printing - first year shown

1998   1999   2000   2001   2002   2003   2004   2005

"I bless you, Father,
Lord of heaven and earth,
from hiding these things
from the learned and the clever,
and revealing them to little children.
Yes, Father, for that
is what it has pleased you to do."

(Lk 10:21 and Mt 11:25)

Table of Contents

Foreword

Perhaps you are smiling to yourself at seeing the two terms "mysticism" and "little children" placed in juxtaposition. One does not ordinarily look for mystics among little children. Go ahead and smile if you will, but do so in wonderment. It is Jesus himself who assures us that *the Father, Lord of heaven and earth, has hidden from the learned and the clever those things he has revealed to little children.*[1] Revealed? Yes. Revealed refers to "those things" that go beyond anything we can conceive, imagine, or desire. Here we find ourselves at the core of "the mystery of God." And that is what mysticism is.

Mysticism is authentic to the extent that the experiences and messages of those who are called "the great explorers of God" include and respect the mode of thought of these "little ones." Or better yet, mysticism is basically the same as living, and so, there are many simple Christians who do

---

[1] In the text that follows, the words of Christ in the New Testament and those of God in the Old are italicized without quotation marks. Other quotations appear in regular type and are set off as quotations.

not keep a spiritual journal, yet live quite simply and generously "those things" that they received at baptism that enable them to say with St. Paul, "I live, yet it is no longer I, but Christ who lives within me" (Gal 2:20).

Whoever you are, whatever you do, the mysticism of the little ones is within reach of your heart, of your life. That is God's gift to you.

So, let us stroll together through the garden of the Gospel gathering some of these flowers of God at random, some of these mysterious and marvelous things Jesus once spoke about and which he continues to speak about today.

Our bouquet, I can assure you, will be more harmonious, more heady than the most beautiful bouquets arranged by the hands of men.

Biblical Abbreviations

OLD TESTAMENT

Genesis	Gn	Nehemiah	Ne	Baruch	Ba
Exodus	Ex	Tobit	Tb	Ezekiel	Ezk
Leviticus	Lv	Judith	Jdt	Daniel	Dn
Numbers	Nb	Esther	Est	Hosea	Ho
Deuteronomy	Dt	1 Maccabees	1 M	Joel	Jl
Joshua	Jos	2 Maccabees	2 M	Amos	Am
Judges	Jg	Job	Jb	Obadiah	Ob
Ruth	Rt	Psalms	Ps	Jonah	Jon
1 Samuel	1 S	Proverbs	Pr	Micah	Mi
2 Samuel	2 S	Ecclesiastes	Ec	Nahum	Na
1 Kings	1 K	Song of Songs	Sg	Habakkuk	Hab
2 Kings	2 K	Wisdom	Ws	Zephaniah	Zp
1 Chronicles	1 Ch	Sirach	Si	Haggai	Hg
2 Chronicles	2 Ch	Isaiah	Is	Malachi	Ml
Ezra	Ezr	Jeremiah	Jr	Zechariah	Zc
		Lamentations	Lm		

NEW TESTAMENT

Matthew	Mt	Ephesians	Eph	Hebrews	Heb
Mark	Mk	Philippians	Ph	James	Jm
Luke	Lk	Colossians	Col	1 Peter	1 P
John	Jn	1 Thessalonians	1 Th	2 Peter	2 P
Acts	Ac	2 Thessalonians	2 Th	1 John	1 Jn
Romans	Rm	1 Timothy	1 Tm	2 John	2 Jn
1 Corinthians	1 Cor	2 Timothy	2 Tm	3 John	3 Jn
2 Corinthians	2 Cor	Titus	Tt	Jude	Jude
Galatians	Gal	Philemon	Phm	Revelation	Rv

AS A LITTLE CHILD

1

Who are these "Little Ones"?

The Greek word *nêpioi* that St. Matthew (11:25) and St. Luke (10:21) use in texts they share in common has a very exact meaning. The *nêpioi* are the newly-born. Even more significant is the fact that this word is found nowhere else in the New Testament and appears only once in the Old. Therefore, it is easy to see that the two evangelists had "newly-born" infants in mind when they composed their texts.

Jesus' insistence on this word is astonishing when we see him use it when he praises his Father *for having revealed these things to little children.* He had just sent the seventy-two disciples in pairs to all the places where he himself had planned to visit. What was their mission? To announce to the people that *the Kingdom of God is very near you.* Sending them out this way, like lambs among wolves, there was reason to fear for the outcome. But surprise! The mission was successful and the missionaries returned "rejoicing." Their word had been effective.

Even though the people who heard the disciples preach were not new-born infants, when they heard the word the disciples brought them they were "born" to a new life. They became "like little children"; they began to live the life of Jesus "who was among them."

Now, at this very time Jesus was at odds with the Pharisees, scribes and doctors of the Law — in short, with *the learned and clever* of Israel, that is, with those who had refused to accept the very same word that those who heard the disciples had accepted, namely that the kingdom of God was very near to them.

But wait a minute. When we put all of this in the context of the heartfelt prayer that Jesus made to his Father, are we not in danger of minimizing the intensity of that prayer? Don't we risk subordinating its meaning to an event of lesser importance that is described in the Gospel? Are we not raising it to more importance than it deserves by attributing to it some absolute value? Far from it! First of all, because rejecting "the mysteries of Christ" on the part of "the learned and clever" is a continuous fact in the history of evangelization; that is so today as it was then. But more especially because Jesus pointed out to us many times what the only road is by which we can enter, with the Father's grace, into faith and have access to life: *In truth I tell you, unless you change and become like little children you will never enter the Kingdom of Heaven* (Mt 18:3).

Even more eloquent an answer to this objection is his own example: Did not he enter the world of men as a new-born baby? And were not the first who adored him simple-hearted shepherds? And did not they hear the voice of the Angel: "I bring you news of great joy, a joy to be shared with the whole people. Today in the town of David a Savior has been born to you; he is Christ the Lord. And here is a sign to you, you will find a baby wrapped in swaddling clothes and lying in a manger" (Lk 2:10-12). The new-born infant will grow and will preach the Good News of Bethlehem to the crowds; he will, so to speak, hold on to the nostalgia of that time when he was merely a newly-born babe lying in a manger, and he will invite those around him to rediscover the child within themselves. *Anyone who welcomes a little child such as this in my name, welcomes me; and anyone who welcomes me, welcomes not me but the one who sent me* (Mk 9:37).

The *nêpioi* are the newly-born, the "born again," those who keep (or rediscover) in their own hearts the first bloom of new-born babes.

2

"You are the Teacher of Israel, and you do not know these things"

John 3:10

The learned and clever were not all averse to Jesus' teaching, but group pressure was so strong that those who were attracted to him did not dare admit it, at least not in the light of day. It was night when Nicodemus, a doctor of the Law, "a leader of the Jews" came to Jesus. "Rabbi, we know that you have come from God as a teacher; for no one could perform the signs that you do unless God were with him." But it was not enough to listen, even with goodwill, to the teachings of Jesus, to admire him as a Master who came from God. One had to "live" the Master's word. His revelation is a call to a new life: *The words I have spoken to you are spirit and they are life* (Jn 6:63). Jesus does not ease into the subject nor does he pay any attention to the highest praise that Nicodemus gives him, but he answers: *In all truth I tell you, no one can see the Kingdom of God without being born from above.* Nicodemus does not understand, and he responds ironically: "How can anyone who is already old be born? Is it possible to go back into the womb again and be born?" Jesus becomes more explicit: *No one can enter the Kingdom of God without being born through water and the Spirit.* Then he comments on this statement by explaining that he is speaking of a re-birth according to the Spirit. *What is born of human nature is human; what is born of the Spirit is spirit. Do not be surprised when I say: You must be born from above.* Nicodemus questions him further: "How is that possible?" And Jesus answers: *You are the Teacher of Israel, and you do not know these things!*

Yes, that was astounding. Here was a doctor of the Law, a man familiar with Scripture who should have been aware of that breath of renewal that whispered throughout the Old Testament. He had read countless times the soul-stirring appeals to conversion that Isaiah, Ezekiel and so many prophets made to the Hebrew people: *Shake off all the sins you have committed against me, and make yourselves a new heart and a new spirit* (Ezk 18:31). *Then you will live; a new world will be established: You shall be my people and I will be your God* (Ezk 36:28). The Precursor John the Baptist claimed that with the coming of Jesus a new world "has arrived." But this was exactly what the "learned" and the "clever" obstinately set themselves against. How could anyone believe that the son of a carpenter from Nazareth was inaugurating a new world? After his conversion, Paul of Tarsus would grasp that Jesus is "the New Adam," that he and he alone was the one announced by the prophets, and that Christians should "put on the New Man that has been created on God's principles, in the uprightness and holiness of the truth" (Eph 4:24); then they will become "a new creature who will be able to begin to live a new life" (Rm 6:4).

Jesus gives an extended answer to Nicodemus's question. What he says is difficult because many of "these things" will not take on their meaning until after his Passion and Resurrection. But at least Jesus succeeds in mapping out for Nicodemus the direction that will lead him to reflect upon the great mystery of God's infinite love. And the honest doctor in Israel will let Jesus' words sink in — he will be re-born.

3

"These things…"

One must admit that this plural — it is neuter in Greek — is a bit vague, but the vagueness of the term enables us to see that either the "things" it describes are themselves imprecise or that there is no term for them in our human language. It is the second hypothesis that we will take up here: we do not have the words that capture divine reality; it goes beyond our intelligence. Revelation speaks to faith.

Jesus tries however to make Nicodemus understand what is essential. The doctor asks him: "How can that be possible?" Jesus responds with words whose exact meaning are beyond one who has no idea of the Trinity, but whose thinking is pointed in that direction: *For this is how God loved the world; he gave his only Son, so that everyone who believes in him may not perish, but have eternal life* (Jn 3:16). Does Nicodemus understand that, and to what extent does he understand? We will come back to him later on at Golgotha, at the time the Crucified is placed in the tomb.

We have at our disposal the precious lights of the New Testament to enable us to ascertain with more clarity Jesus' response to Nicodemus and in the light-and-shade of faith we can delineate the Father's marvelous gift.

"These things" — it means first of all, God telling us about eternal life, telling us about his own life. *And eternal life is this: to know you the only true God* ["to know" in the Biblical sense, that is, to have a living experience of someone] *and to know Jesus Christ whom you have sent* (Jn 17:3). And Jesus came to affirm: *I have come so that they may have life and have it to the full* (Jn 10:10). For our part, we ask, "How can this be?" By becoming members of the reality which is "the Body of Christ," "through water and the Holy Spirit" (Baptism), by becoming his brothers and sisters, and therefore the (adopted) sons of the Father. The result is that every Christian can say with St. Paul: "It is no longer I, but Christ living in me" (Gal 2:10).

This is the wonderful "metamorphosis" of our mortal life into life eternal. A new status is thereby created for us, a "vocation" to which St. John, giving up the neuter expression — these things — designates with a substantive that is more precise — *Unum* (one). We are quite accurately plunged into the vital life of the Trinity. Jesus said to his disciples: *On that day you will know that I am in my Father and you in me and I in you* (Jn 14:20). And also: *Anyone who loves me will keep*

*my word, and my Father will love him, and we shall
come to him and make a home in him* (Jn 14:23). One
home where an exchange of life takes place: God
living in us and we living in God.

This extraordinary unity of each Christian
with God is the foundation of the unity among
us, as Jesus prayed a short time before he entered
into his Passion: *May they be one, just as, Father,
you are in me and I am in you, so that they may be
one in us* (Jn 17:21).

Jesus did not reveal to his apostles "these
things," these divine realities until his earthly life
was coming to an end. In his instructions to the
crowds during the three years of his public life, he
used language that was more matter-of-fact, more
adaptable to their day-to-day experience. He used
parables. By taking examples from things that the
ordinary people saw and heard, the Father revealed
to them, little by little and in their heart of hearts,
"things" that their eyes had never seen and their
ears had never heard.

4

"He would not speak to them except in parables"

Mark 4:34

When he preached to the people, Jesus used the parable as the chief means — along with miracles — to orientate them toward the "things of the Kingdom." In his manner of proceeding, there was a real pedagogical method. He presented an image for the crowds that was straight-on, so to speak: *Let those who have ears to hear, hear.* Then he would comment on the meaning of his parables to the disciples: "Using many parables like these, he spoke the word to them, so far as they were capable of understanding it. He would not speak to them except in parables, but he explained everything to his disciples when they were by themselves" (Mk 4:33-34). Finally, it was to his apostles alone that he addressed the topics of his last conversations and in these he did away with pictorial language or used it as the point of departure for a clear revelation. "His disciples said, 'Now you are

speaking plainly and not using veiled language'"
(Jn 16:29). Still later, the Holy Spirit would have
to be sent to make them understand "those things"
that no human language could encompass.

The Gospel parables are as varied as were
the lives of those ordinary folks who pressed in
around Jesus to hear what he had to say. Many of
the parables deal with the world of plants, not just
because Jesus' auditors were country people, but
because plants share in the mystery of human life
— they are born, grow, produce fruit, wilt, die and
are then reborn. Birth and rebirth! The central
mystery of life! Everyone knows the parable of the
sower: *Of its own accord the land produces first the
shoot, then the ear, then the full grain in the ear* (Mk
4:28), and the parable of the mustard seed: *the
smallest of all the seeds on earth. Yet once it is sown it
grows into the biggest shrub of them all and puts out
big branches so that the birds of the air can shelter in
its shade* (Mk 4:30-32). Moreover, Jesus, "the son
of the carpenter," who himself is a carpenter and
would one day know how to die on "the wood of
the cross" for the salvation of the world, also shows
a preference for the tree, which plays such an important role in the Old Testament.

Within this world of grains, shrubs, and
trees, Jesus seems to have reserved a particularly
significant place for the vine when he teaches with
greater precision about the "things of the King-

dom." In the Old Testament the vine was the symbol of Israel's destiny: God loved his vine; he dug the soil around it, cleared away the stones, protected it, but it yielded only sour grapes, and so the Lord took away the hedge that protected it so that the animals could graze on it, and he knocked down the wall so that it could be trampled on. *I will lay it waste, unpruned, uncultivated; overgrown by the briar and the thorn* (Is 5:6). During the discourse at the Last Supper, Jesus identified himself as the vine planted by the Father: *I am the true vine, and my Father is the vinedresser* (Jn 15:1). The disciples are the branches of this vine. Everything that deals with salvation, with the "re-birth" of humanity, is focused on this simple vision: one and the same sap circulates from the stock to the branches; if a branch is no longer fed by the sap, it withers and is only good for burning; on the other hand, if a branch "dwells in," that is, is united to the sap, it bears fruit, and if the Father prunes the branches it is only *to make them bear more fruit* (Jn 15:1-9). There are many more reasons for Jesus' predilection for this symbol of the vine, the most important of which was this: the whole Bible sings of the joy the fruit of the vine — wine — gives to the heart of man, and in his last hours on earth, Jesus will raise wine well beyond its symbolic value; he will make it the reality of his Blood in the eucharistic mystery. Over the cup he will say: *Drink from this all of you, for this is my blood, the blood of the new covenant, poured out for many for the forgiveness of sins* (Mt 26:27-28). It will become the beverage of the eternal banquet.

5

"There were many other signs…"

John 20:30

Jesus evidently did not perform his miracles for the "newly-born." For the newly-born babe everything is new, everything is "wonderment." But the adult who has come to know "the natural laws" clearly distinguishes between what is consistent with, what is possible for, and what is contrary to nature's laws. Whatever contradicts these laws goes beyond his understanding. Faced with factual events for which his reason has no explanation, he is like a new-born babe — he is born to a new world.

The Gospel is full of instances when Jesus performed actions that disrupted the natural laws. He did not work any miracle for the sake of the spectacular. Rather, he performed them "so that you may believe that Jesus is the Christ, the Son of God, and that believing this you may have life through his name" (Jn 20:30). So then, Jesus' purpose for performing miracles is clear. His miracles that are described in the Gospel are always in the realm of the religious. They cannot and should not be separated from his Word. His miracles are a "sign."

The quality of the sign can be seen most clearly in a number of these miracles.

For example, there is the healing of the paralytic of Capernaum. The crowds of people pressing in on Jesus were so great that in order to get the sick man to him, four men had to let him down through the roof. Jesus said to the man lying there before him: *My child, your sins are forgiven.* The poor man did not expect to be absolved; he was hoping to be cured! Some scribes in the crowd who witnessed what Jesus said were scandalized: "Who but God can forgive sins?" And Jesus answered: *Which of these is easier to say, "Your sins are forgiven" or to say "Get up, pick up your stretcher, and walk"? But to prove to you that the Son of man has authority to forgive sins on earth* — he then said to the paralytic — *I order you: get up, pick up your stretcher, and go off home.* The crowd was astonished, and they remarked, "We have never seen anything like this" (Mk 2:1-12).

Then there was the raising to life of the son of the widow of Nain. The reaction of everyone in this case was to give "glory to God." Jesus happened to be coming toward the village of Nain when he met a number of people carrying out a

dead man to be buried, the only son of his wid-
owed mother. Jesus felt sorry for the poor woman.
To raise a dead man to life, to make one reborn to
life — What a symbol of a new "Kingdom" that
was! What a sign it was of who Jesus is! The crowd
in the funeral procession realized well enough what
it meant. "God has visited his people," they said.
"And this view of him spread throughout all Judaea
and all over the countryside" (Lk 7:16-17). What
"signs" a person will discover reflecting on the
miracles Jesus performed!

There is one other fact that should attract
our attention. Usually, just before Jesus performs
one of his miracles, he "blesses" the Father in a
fervent prayer. For instance, before raising his
friend Lazarus from the dead, he said: *I bless you,
Father, for hearing my prayer. I myself knew that you
hear me always, but I speak for the sake of all these
who are standing around me so that they may believe
it was you who sent me* (Jn 11:42).

Here is another example. While he was in
prison, John the Baptist heard about the first
"works" of Jesus of Nazareth. He sent some of his
followers to ask him, "Are you the one who is to
come, or are we to expect someone else?" To which
Jesus replied: *Go back and tell John what you have
seen and heard: the blind see again, the lame walk,
those suffering from virulent skin-diseases are cleansed,
and the deaf hear, the dead are raised to life, the good*

news is proclaimed to the poor (Lk 7:18-23). According to Isaiah these are precisely the signs that tell that "the days of salvation" have arrived.

6

"In no one in Israel have I found faith as great as this"

Matthew 8:10

After listening to Jesus' parables, hearing his teaching and seeing his miracles, the crowd was divided. There were some who believed in him and some who did not. "His words caused a fresh division among the Jews. Many said, 'He is possessed, he is raving; why do you listen to him?' Others said, 'These are not the words of a man possessed by a devil; could a devil open the eyes of the blind?'" (Jn 10:19-21).

But what could have been the faith of these first believers? It certainly was not the faith which we find in the whole, polished, detailed creed that we profess today — a profession of belief composed after our Savior's Passion, Resurrection, and Ascension... and with the light of the Holy Spirit. It was only a simple — and we do not mean simplistic — instinctive, and to some extent, populist attachment to someone who spoke "like no one ever spoke," who did things "that no one had ever done," whose person radiated authority, goodness, hope, love. Good people, the "pure of heart," and "poor of spirit" felt something even more; they realized that somehow they were face to face with truth. "God is with him," as Nicodemus put it. God with his power, goodness, mercy and wisdom was with him. "'When Christ comes, will he perform more signs than this man has?' they asked" (Jn 7:31). This question sums up well the attitude of those who believed in him. Was it an elementary faith, still imperfect, yet centered on the person of Jesus? Indeed it was.

But to "bring oneself" to this wonderful person Jesus, a person still needed something further; he had to be drawn by the Father. Nonetheless the profound orientation toward the mystery of Christ is already present in these first believers.

We can now better understand the praise — "Your faith has saved you" — that Jesus bestows on certain persons in the Gospel: the blind man of Jericho (Mk 10:52), the grateful leper (Lk 17:19). And everyone can make his own the words of the father of the epileptic demoniac: "I do have faith. Help my lack of faith!" (Mk 9:23).

It is in this attitude that we see an essential characteristic of the faith of those men and women for whom Jesus worked a miracle: their humility; their belief that they themselves could do nothing but that Jesus could do all. This humility is particularly evident in two of the miracles we find in the Gospel. By expressing her satisfaction with scraps from the table that were meant for dogs, the Canaanite woman obtained Jesus' healing for her daughter. *It is not fair to take the children's food and throw it to little dogs*, Jesus had said. "She retorted: 'Ah yes, Lord, but even little dogs eat the scraps that fall from their masters' table.'" Then Jesus answered her, *Woman, you have great faith. Let it be done for you as you wish* (Mt 15:26-28).

Then there is the faith shown by the centurion of Jerusalem who came to Jesus asking him to heal his servant: "Sir, I am not worthy to have you under my roof; just give the word and my servant will be cured." As a result, Jesus was "astonished" and he in turn addressed the Jews who were following him: *In truth I tell you, in no one in Israel have I found faith as great as this* (Mt 8:10).

The Canaanite woman and the centurion were not of the "sons of Israel."

7

"You have hidden these things from the learned and the clever"

Luke 10:21

Let us admit that this statement of Jesus is mysterious. It can even be taken the wrong way. There
are other texts, however, that echo its meaning:
*No one can come to me unless drawn by the Father
who sent me* (Jn 6:44). Does God have preferences?
Does he choose arbitrarily? Does he designate
some to hear the things of the Kingdom and hold
back revelation from others? A text from Luke
(8:10) can even lead us to believe that if Jesus used
parables in his teaching, it was only that some
people "may look but not perceive, listen but not
understand." A key to this problem can be found
in the Acts of the Apostles (28:27) where the harsh
text of Isaiah (6:10), which is also cited by Matthew (13:14) and John (12:40), is given. Here is
Paul's version of it: "God has given them a slug-
gish spirit, unseeing eyes and inattentive ears, and
they are still like that today" (Rm 11:8).

If God "hides" the things of the Kingdom from some people, it is because instead of being open to truth, upright, decent — in short, instead of being genuinely honest, according to their vocation as being created in "the image of God," they become hard-hearted with pride and deceit. They, not God, are responsible for their alienation from God.

This is exactly the case with "the learned and the clever" from whom God "hides" the things of the Kingdom. How would they be able to see in Jesus the one sent by God since they "know" that the Law does "not allow" the paralytic at the Pool of Bethesda to carry his sleeping-mat on the Sabbath, as "the man who cured" him told him to do? Or how could he, who came from Galilee, be the Christ (they were ignorant of the circumstances of Jesus' birth; for them he was Jesus of Nazareth)? "Would the Christ come from Galilee? Doesn't Scripture say that the Christ must be descended from David and come from Bethlehem?" (Jn 7:41). Or how could a blasphemer, who "spoke of God as his own Father" (Jn 5:18), or who forgave sins (Mt 9:3), be Christ, the one sent by God?

And not only were "those who knew" the Law incapable of believing but they also tried to prevent others from believing as well. They exercised a tyranny of fear over the crowds — witness how they treated the parents of the man born blind (Jn 9:22). It was a tyranny that was so powerful that it even extended to the community leaders themselves. "And yet there were many who did believe in him," reported St. John, "even among the leading men, but they did not admit it because of the Pharisees and for fear of being banned from the synagogue" (Jn 12:42). If the Pharisees caused such fear, they in turn were fearful of the Romans: "If we let him go on this way everybody will believe in him, and the Romans will come and suppress the Holy Place and our nation." To this Caiaphas, the high priest that year, answered: "You do not seem to have grasped the situation at all; you fail to see that it is to your advantage that one man should die for the people, rather than that the whole nation should perish" (Jn 11:47-50).

How far were these learned and wise men from the simplicity of newly-born babes and those like them! How could the things of the Kingdom take root in such hard, calloused hearts? To reveal these things would be useless. We are face to face here with the mystery of sin that shuts a person off from God.

8

"Go, make disciples of the nations; Baptize…"

Matthew 28:19-20

There is no action greater or more all-encompassing for man than his baptism: no stage in his life is more divine. It is in baptism that he is reborn to the life for which God created man in the very beginning, his true life, his eternal life. We live this reality in the mystery of faith. It is the basic mystery and everything we call "mystical" must be integrated into the mysticism of baptism in order for it to be genuine.

Except in cases of emergency, the baptismal ceremony takes place in three stages which are closely connected.

1. A conversion, a reversal of life: the catechumen (or in the case of an infant, the parents and godparents) renounce Satan and sin and "are joined to Jesus Christ forever";

2. A profession of faith in the revelation of the Scriptures;

3. The Church's minister "plunges" the one to be baptized into the water "in the name of the Father, and of the Son, and of the Holy Spirit" and anoints him with holy oil.

It is simple, but it is the simplicity of God himself, like the Creator's "let it be done," or the priest's "this is" over the bread and wine.

In fact, this simple act is a divine re-creation at the very depths of a person's being. The one baptized becomes a "new man," a "new creation" (Gal 6:15). He is born "not of human stock," but now he is born "from God himself" (Jn 1:13).

What is this new life?

Essentially it consists in the baptized being "one," from that moment on, with the Risen Jesus Christ and, as a result of that unity, becoming a "child of God." Just as Christ lives the life given to him by the Father, so the newly baptized lives Christ's life. Truly, he can now say, "My Father..." He abides in Christ as Christ abides in the Father.

Being made one with Christ means being introduced into the intimate life of the Trinity. We are carried along by him in the great current of the infinite love flowing from the heart of the Father — a love, first for Christ, then for "all of those who believe in the Son," and, finally through their fidelity this love returns to the Father and glorifies him. The activator of this wonderful movement is the Holy Spirit. "God is love," says St. John, and "this is the revelation of God's love for us, that God sent his only Son into the world that we might have life through him… If God loved us so much, we too should love each other" (1 Jn 4:9-11). St. Paul's words are borne out in us: "It is in him that we live, and move, and have our being" (Ac 17:28).

It is evident that this re-birth is "God's mystery"; however it is not beyond our experience. "Baptism," says St. Peter, is "an appeal to God for a clean conscience through the resurrection of Jesus Christ" (1 P 3:21). We experience this "salvation" to some extent in our conscious life when, docile to the impulses of the Spirit, we "metamorphosize" (it is St. Paul's expression) the human imperfections of our consciousness through stirrings of love and when, in our daily moral struggles, we feel the strength and efficacy of our filial prayer.

This re-birth is, in fact, the consecration of our whole being to God. It is a unique, fundamental, primordial consecration. Vatican II teaches this with great insistence: "The participation in liturgical celebrations by the Christian people as 'a chosen race, a royal priesthood, a holy nation, a purchased people' (1 P 2:9), is their right and duty by reason of their baptism" (*Sacrosanctum Concilium*, 144). Through baptism a person "has died to sin and has been consecrated to God" (*Lumen Gentium*, 44). "The special consecration that religious make through their vows is deeply rooted in their baptismal consecration and... provides an ampler manifestation of it" (*Perfectae Caritatis*, 5).

If you only knew the gift that God is offering, Jesus said to the Samaritan woman. He says these same words to us today.

9

"We have been joined to Christ"

Romans 6:5

Our unity (*Unum*) with the Risen Christ goes so far beyond what we can possibly understand or desire that it will be useful for us to consider, first of all, the few words we have that Jesus spoke during his earthly life and then, what some of his apostles said after he had departed.

Before his Passion and Resurrection, Jesus hardly ever made any reference to this mystery. However, during his Last Supper discourse, he depicted for us the symbol of the vine and branches (Jn 15:1-9). Then twice afterwards, he used a consciously obscure expression of great meaning: to be "with me" (*Mecum*). With these two words, he gave an accurate description of the image of the vine and its branches.

How does he defeat the resistance of Peter on Holy Thursday as he prepares to wash the feet of his apostles? He says: *If I do not wash you, you can have no share with me.* Before such a threat,

Peter backs down and gives in (Jn 13:8).

On Golgotha, the repentant thief who, like himself, is dying on a cross, pleads with him: "Jesus, remember me when you come into your kingdom." Jesus promises: *In truth I tell you, today you will be with me in paradise* (Lk 23:42-43).

In the final confidence to his apostles, Jesus twice defines the meaning of this "with me," and in doing so he equates it with divine love itself. *I am not alone*, he said, *because the Father is with me* (Jn 16:32). And he prayed to his Father: *Father, I want those you have given me to be with me where I am, so that they may always see my glory which you have given me because you loved me before the foundation of the world* (Jn 17:24).

Among the apostles and evangelists, it was St. Paul who seems to have been most taken by these "*mecum*" expressions of Jesus. We will not speak of his beautiful image of the "graft" (Rm 11:24), but will stress how he afterwards created a whole vocabulary to enable us to understand that through baptism we become part of the same "plant" as Christ; that we are "joined to him" (Rm 6:5). "So by our baptism into his death we were buried with him, so that as Christ was raised from the dead by the Father's glorious power, we too should begin living a new life" (Rm 6:4). Later contrasting words flow from his pen: *commortui/ convivemus*, die with/live with (1 Tm 2:11); *conspulti/consurrexistis*, buried with/raised up (Col

2:12); *compatimur/conglorificemur*, share in suffering/share in glory (Rm 8:17). And this is the rationale of the mystery of this new life: "because you have died, now the life you have is hidden with Christ in God. But when Christ is revealed" — and he is your life — "you too, will be revealed with him in glory" (Col 3:3).

Anyone who is not with me is against me, and anyone who does not gather with me scatters (Mt 12:30).

What limitless horizons exist for those who are "with Christ"! Such is the response of the God of love to our humble and fragile promise, "I attach myself to Jesus Christ forever." But does this gift of God risk absorbing our heart in a selfish possessiveness? Absolutely not. It drives us, compels us, to bind ourselves more closely to our fellow human beings, to be "with them." It is in the one Spirit (the Spirit of the Father and of Jesus) that all of us have been baptized into the one Body. Through our baptism we are members of the same body, the head of which is Christ. This is the paradox of divine love: the more it is intensified in us, the more it demands that we love one another. There is a continuous exchange between the love of God and the love of neighbor. The one strengthens the other; they are two aspects of the same love.

10

"If I am without love…"

1 Corinthians 13:1-3

During the course of their mission, the seventy-two disciples performed many marvels in the name of the Lord; they even delivered people possessed by evil spirits! When they returned they gave Jesus an account of their exploits. In rejoicing with them over what they had accomplished, he put everything in its proper perspective: *Do not rejoice that the spirits submit to you; rejoice instead that your names are written in heaven* (Lk 10:20). In other words, your treasure is not your charisms; it is your belonging to "the things of the Kingdom." The former depends on the latter.

St. Paul will have to call this same truth to the attention of his Christians. There was an abundance of signs and prodigies that accompanied the preaching of the Gospel in the earliest days. It was inevitable that a number of the newly converted pagans attached more importance to preternatural gifts than to the interior mystery of their baptism. Paul forcefully warned the Corinthians of this fact: "Though I command languages both human and angelic — if I speak without love, I am no more than a gong booming or a cymbal clashing. And though I have the power of prophecy to penetrate all mysteries and knowledge, and though I have all the faith necessary to move mountains — if I am without love, I am nothing. Though I should give away to the poor all that I possess, and even give up my body to be burned — if I am without love, it will do me no good whatever" (1 Cor 13:1-3).

What then is love? It is participation in the life of Christ and, through Christ, in the life of the Trinity which we receive through baptism. It is on a par with faith and hope, but whereas faith and hope will be reabsorbed in the eternal light of seeing God face to face, love, or charity as it is also called, will endure. Meanwhile, let it motivate more our daily lives each day: "Love is always patient and kind; love is never jealous; love is not boastful or conceited, it is never rude and never seeks its own advantage, it does not take offense or store grievances. Love does not rejoice at wrongdoing, but finds its joy in the truth. It is always ready to make allowances, to trust, to hope and to endure whatever comes" (1 Cor 13:4-7). St. Paul puts a great emphasis on the "small" domestic virtues; and he always ties them to this source within us, which is love: "Brothers," he writes to the

Philippians (4:8-9), "let your minds be filled with everything that is true, everything that is honorable, everything that is upright and pure, everything that we love and admire — with whatever is good and praiseworthy… Then the God of peace will be with you." All of these things are the fruit of the Spirit who animates and frees the baptized (Gal 5:22); it is the mysticism of baptism.

If such is the case, let us define more accurately what we mean by the word mystic. Let us not restrict the word to those whom God favors with extraordinary insights, prodigious gifts, exceptional powers. Let us not be too quick to cut up the ascetic and the mystic into neat little categories, into "purgative, illuminative, and unitive" ways. The ordinary, run-of-the mill baptized Christians can qualify as mystics, provided they live their day-to-day family, professional, and social lives "at the factory and in the fields, in their shops and in their homes" (St. Francis de Sales), as the Spirit commands, counsels, and inspires them, and provided that they do their utmost to live their baptismal promises each moment of the day. Such Christians are able to say with St. Paul: "I am alive; yet it is no longer I, but Christ living in me. The life that I am now living, subject to the limitation of human nature, I am living in faith, faith in the Son of God who loved me and gave himself up for me" (Gal 2:20-21).

11

"But you, who do you say that I am?"

Mark 8:29

Jesus then is the very center, the "keystone," so to speak, of God's plan for the rebirth of mankind and of each of the baptized. How? Why? Who is Jesus?

In the eyes of his contemporaries, he was Jesus of Nazareth, "the son of Joseph the carpenter" (Lk 4:22), a carpenter himself, and the son of Mary (Mk 6:22). Such is the way that he would identify himself to the guards who would come to arrest him at Gethsemane. The Incarnation was no myth: by it the eternal Word took on our condition: "becoming as human beings are; and being in every way like a human being" (Ph 2:7).

Those who came to believe in him, his teachings, and the signs he performed during the course of his public life had an inkling that this man was more than just a man, that God was with him. They called him "Prophet," even "Messiah." Indeed, Peter went so far as to call him "the Christ of God." But all of these expressions were tainted with a certain ambiguity: this Messiah, this Christ, was still in their minds one who would be a temporal ruler who would restore the kingdom of Israel, the "liberator of the chosen people." It was only as the Passion drew near that Jesus would clearly reveal to his disciples his identity with the Father: *Anyone who has seen me has seen the Father; I am in the Father and the Father is in me... I came from the Father and have come into the world... Now, Father, glorify me with that glory I had with you before ever the world existed... The Paraclete, the Holy Spirit whom the Father will send in my name, will instruct you in everything, and remind you of all I told you* (Jn 14:9, 10; 16:28; 17:5; 14:25).

And in fact, after the Resurrection and Ascension, Jesus' identity with the Father will be revealed more fully to us through the Acts and Letters of the Apostles. He has been "raised on high" by the Father, who "gave him the name which is above all other names" (Ph 2:9), that is, the Father has given Jesus universal dominion over every creature. He is the "image of the invisible God" (Col 1:15). "In him, in bodily form, lives divinity" (Col 2:9). That is to say that the divinity lives corporally, in the reality of his risen human body and also in the reality of his mystical body of which he is the head. Paul expresses this mystery with a most beautiful image wherein his ardent faith in the mystery of the Incarnation becomes apparent. He begs the Ephesians to preserve "unity of faith and knowledge of the Son of God" and to achieve "mature manhood, to the extent of Christ's full stature" (Eph 4:13).

And so, how do we answer the question Jesus once posed to his apostles and which he poses today to every baptized person: *And you, who do you say that I am?* Ever since the day of our baptism, we have said: "I join myself to Jesus Christ forever." What Jesus Christ? Doubtless each one of us has given a different answer. Each one is attracted, according to his particular temperament or to the grace he has received, to a different aspect of Christ. For some, he is the friend; for others the spouse; for others, the leader, or the head of the Mystical Body. The essential is that, apart from these inevitable differences, each answer to the question agrees on one single point. St. John states precisely, and in a magnificent way, what this point is: "We are declaring to you what we have seen and heard, so that you too may share our life" (1 Jn 1:1-3). Jesus is the Eternal Word, Jesus is God made man, Jesus lived, suffered, and died for men, Jesus was raised up by the Father — that is "who he is" for all the baptized. "He is everything and he is in everything," as St. Paul says (Col 3:11). As the Seer of Revelation saw him, he is the Lamb "as sacrificed." This Lamb, before whom all the angels and all living creatures prostrate themselves in worship, bears the wounds of his Passion.

12

"There in their presence he was transfigured"

Mark 9:2

One day, however, even before his resurrection, Jesus lifted a corner of the veil that hid the identity of the Word made flesh. He manifested something of his mystery no longer in parables, signs, and words, but in action.

It was the pinnacle moment of his earthly life. At Caesarea Philippi, Peter had confessed, "You are the Christ!" and Jesus clearly announced for the first time his Passion and Resurrection; he stated explicitly to anyone who wanted to follow him: *If anyone wants to be a follower of mine, let him renounce himself, take up his cross and come after me.* Then he announced that the coming of the Kingdom was imminent. His transfiguration took place six days later (Mt 17:1).

Jesus went "up a high mountain" (Tabor, according to tradition) "to pray" (Lk 9:28). He "took with him" three of his apostles: Peter (the leader of the group), John (the disciple Jesus loved), and James (the first of the apostles who would give witness to Jesus by shedding his blood). In making the climb toward the top, Jesus was simply their ordinary day-to-day companion, a man among men, even though his actions showed that "God is with him."

However, during his prayer, Jesus was suddenly transfigured: "his face shone like the sun and his clothes became as dazzling as light" (Mt 17:2). Jesus retained his human face but it had become a face that reflected his divinity; he still wore ordinary clothes, but now these clothes seemed to be made of light. This change in Christ is not like the stalk that ripens into heads of grain, nor like the chrysalis that turns into a butterfly. It is the manifestation of what *is*, as if one were suddenly to pull aside a cover draped over a hidden light. The real question is not, "How could that come about?" but rather: "How is it that such glory was manifested for but a moment?" This is the mystery of the Word Incarnate.

Jesus and the three apostles were not alone on the mountain. Moses and Elijah were also present "appearing with him in glory." What were they speaking about, immersed in all this light? They were "speaking of his passage, which he was about to fulfill in Jerusalem." They were referring to the Cross, but already it was the glorious Cross.

The scene amazed Peter, James and John — "It is wonderful to be here" — and stirred up in them such pleasant feelings that Peter, not knowing what he was saying, suggested: "Master, let us set up three booths here, one for you, one for Moses and one for Elijah."

Suddenly there appeared a "bright cloud" from which a voice was heard: *This is my Son, my Beloved in whom I am well pleased.* Terrified, the three apostles fell to the ground.

Then everything faded away. The apostles came back to their normal selves and "saw no one but Jesus." He had become once more Jesus the man, their daily companion, whose face and clothing they knew so well.

What a light this was on the personality of the Word made flesh! And, as a by-effect, what a light on our baptism that makes us "sons of God"! Our life is lived on two planes, the "visible" and the "invisible." Two planes that continuously interact with one another during this life, but will fuse into one when "the Lord Jesus Christ will transfigure this wretched body of ours after the fashion of his own glorious body, through the working of the power which he has" (Ph 3:20-21). St. John expresses in a wonderful way this mystery of the baptized: "We are already God's children, but what we shall be in the future has not yet been revealed. We are well aware that when he appears we shall be like him because we shall see him as he really is (1 Jn 3:2). Then our eyes will be able to see the invisible and our ears hear the ineffable.

13

"Pray continually and never lose heart…"

Luke 18:1

Let us come down from the slopes of Tabor and take up our ordinary daily lives. In the midst of all of our difficulties, how do we keep in contact with Jesus who is, according to St. Augustine's all but untranslatable expression, *interior intimo meo, et superior summo meo*, "Deeper in me than my inmost depth and higher than my utmost reach." The way, we know, is "to pray continually."

I hear you say: "But I don't know how to pray." Or, "I find prayer boring; I have too many distractions." Really now, don't you know how imperfectly spoken infants are when they are hungry or thirsty or how they stammer when they "fall down and go boom"? Don't they just cry out to be attended to? Is not this the same advice the Lord gives us: "to pray continually and never lose heart" (Lk 18:1)? And St. Paul is very explicit: "Whatever you say or do, let it be in the name of the

Lord Jesus, giving thanks to God the Father through him" (Col 3:17). Or even more plainly, he writes: "Whatever you eat, then, or drink, and whatever else you do, do it all for the glory of God" (1 Cor 10:31). So?

So, let us simply imitate new born babes; let us call on Jesus like the sick, the infirm, and the desperate whom we meet in the Gospels, "Lord, I want to see… Lord, that I may walk… Lord, come to my aid." And if what we ask for is granted, let us not forget to give thanks, to "bless" his benevolent hand.

In our busy, agitated times, why not put to use the well known "ejaculatory prayers," those darts that shoot forth to the heart of God? Scripture and the liturgy provide us in abundance with many such short prayers. But those that spring forth from within us — or without us, so to speak — are the most opportune.

Eastern Christians have discovered a very useful and time-honored method to unite us to Jesus. It consists in slowly repeating the Gospel invocation that draws Jesus to our heart, "Lord Jesus, Son of God, have mercy on me, a sinner." We can say it with every breath we take; it can become our "breath of life," so that each time we inhale we call on Jesus, the Son of God, to take possession of our heart, and, as we exhale, our sinful nature calls on our Savior's mercy. A great peace then envelops us. Jesus becomes the All of our thoughts and our affections. Normally this prayer becomes more simplified as we repeat it; we come to utter the name "Jesus" alone, and then, with unmoving lips, there is only the silent, luminous Presence in our heart: "Jesus."

After that, do we not become aware of an interior dialogue taking place? It is in this dialogue that we speak to God and he speaks to us. An old peasant from Ars once defined this prayer in a marvelous way. When his sainted pastor, the Curé of Ars, asked him to tell him the secret of his long visits before the Blessed Sacrament, he replied with simplicity: "I just look at him and he looks at me."

Such are the children who can only join their hands and say the word "Jesus"; these "little ones" — who are "neither the learned nor the clever" — simply sigh "Jesus," whenever something goes well or wrong. They are perhaps great mystics and do not even know it. Tremendous faith, hope and love can be packed into this word "Jesus." And the quality of these three virtues in us measures our "attachment to Jesus Christ forever." There is no surer criterion for our true union with God.

Finally, let us not hesitate to make the sign of the cross often, and with reverence. It is the act whereby we affirm that, ever since our baptism, the Holy Trinity dwells within us and that we must treasure the Cross of Jesus.

14

"In Jesus Christ, the Son of God, there was only 'Yes'…"

2 Corinthians 1:19

We should not pray with words alone but with our whole being. We should say "yes" unceasingly to God in every aspect of our life. And that "yes" should be sincere. There is hardly a single sin — pride excepted — that God detests as much as lying. *All you need say is "Yes" if you mean yes, "No" if you mean no* (Mt 5:37). *The Devil,* Christ tells us in St. John's Gospel, *is a liar and the father of lies* (Jn 8:44).

One day St. Paul dipped into his own experience to give us a forceful reminder of how God regards truthfulness. Paul had promised the faithful at Corinth that he would visit them, but then he had to change his plans. Did he "lightly change his mind"? Did he have "yes" and "no" in his head at the same time? The very suggestion was intolerable for an apostle. "As surely as God is trustworthy, what we say to you is not both Yes and

No. The Son of God, Jesus Christ, who was proclaimed to you by us, that is by me and by Silvanus and Timothy, was never Yes-and-No; his nature is all Yes. For in him is found the Yes to all God's promises and therefore it is 'through him' that we answer 'Amen' to give praise to God" (2 Cor 1:18-20). A typical Paul-like jump: he starts off with something terribly ordinary — a canceled visit — and he ends up by revealing to us to a divine mystery. He gives godlike nobility to the simple virtue of being true to one's word.

Our own history in this area of sincerity is not exactly sterling. It is a record all of us share in common. "No man can be relied upon" (Ps 116:11). The whole of the Old Testament is full of instances of Israel's infidelity versus God's fidelity. And how about ourselves? Who among us would dare to say that he has always been faithful to his baptismal promises? Happy those times when, perchance, we have acted like the boy in the parable whose father asked him to go and work in the vineyard and he responded, "I will not go," but afterwards repented what he had said and did as his father asked (Mt 21:28-30). "Who can find a man really worthy of trust?" asks the sage in Proverbs (Pr 20:6).

Actually, can perfect truth be found in anyone here in this life? It seems that truth is not a virtue that we possess fully, but with the aid of the Holy Spirit we can approach it. Jesus said of himself: *I am the Way and the Truth and the Life* (Jn 14:6). If we follow this Way "we walk towards the Truth," as the biblical expression has it, toward a progressive purification of all that is false in us, and this purification is brought about through the influence of Jesus the Truth, whom we have received at baptism (1 P 1:22), who makes us "God-fearing men, trustworthy and incorruptible" (Ex 18:21). This is so because the Father answers the prayer that Jesus made at the eve of his death — *Consecrate them in the truth* (Jn 17:17) — in those who remain faithful in this manner. "What is the truth?" Pilate asked Jesus. The faithful baptized Christian answers: "The truth is Jesus living in me."

Do not think that it is always easy to say "Yes" to our Father's will. It was not always so for Jesus either. As he began his Passion in Gethsemane, he experienced sorrow to the point of death. He knew fear and anguish and cried out to heaven his prayer of distress, *Father, if it be possible, let this cup pass from me.* He said, *Father.* His cry therefore was not a cry of revolt or non-acceptance; it was like the moan of a little one. And even at that moment came forth from his lips his final "Yes": *Nevertheless, not my will but yours be done* (Mt 26:39). The Father's plan would be accomplished.

15

"This is my Body... This is my Blood..."

Luke 22:9

God is simple and his most divine actions are also the most simple. *Unum* — one — suffices to explain the mystery of the Trinity and the mystery of the Mystical Body. Notice particularly how readily he uses the verb "to be," the most common verb in all languages, whenever he wants to define himself, *I am who am.* And so with all of creation: "*Let there be light* and the light came to be." One might say that the God Man employed a characteristic language and style whenever he cured the sick or brought the dead back to life; he used the clearest terms, the briefest imperative: "Get up and walk."

Again, this same simplicity of words and action is evident in what St. Francis de Sales described as "this ineffable mystery that encompasses the unfathomable depths of divine love," that is, the Eucharist: *This is my Body... This is my Blood.*

This simplicity of God's way of acting and

speaking is of the highest importance in the mysticism of little children. If we say, "Baptism is being buried in Christ's Passion, Death, and Resurrection and the Eucharist is the memorial of his Passion, Death and Resurrection," will we be understood by little children and "those who resemble them"? But if we tell them how Jesus managed to reveal to the crowds that he would really, truly, daily remain among us, then we will have a chance of making ourselves understood.

The first reference to the Eucharist took place within the context of an obvious miracle in which Jesus spoke in very concrete terms. It was at Capernaum, at the approach of the Jewish feast of the Passover. In order to feed a crowd of five thousand men who had been following him, Jesus multiplied two barley loaves and five fish that a small boy had with him. The result was that all were filled. Clearly those who had been the beneficiaries of this miracle wanted to follow after such a provider of good things. In fact, they wanted to make him king. Jesus used this popular enthusiasm to reveal something about what he had in mind regarding the Eucharist. *The bread I shall give you is my flesh for the life of the world.* The Jews were not about to understand such a figure of speech in this connection. "How can this man give us his flesh to eat?" they asked. Jesus insisted: *In truth I tell you, if you do not eat the flesh of the Son of Man and drink his blood, you have no life in you... for my flesh is real food and my blood is real drink* (Jn 6:53-55). Too much, too much! "After this, many of his disciples went away and accompanied him no more." Jesus then said to the twelve, *What about you, do you want to go away too?* It was at that moment that Peter, inspired by the Holy Spirit, exclaimed in the name of the rest, "Lord to whom would we go? You have the message of eternal life; and we believe, indeed we have come to know, that you are the Holy One of God" (Jn 6:66-69).

What a prologue to his institution of the Eucharist on Holy Thursday! The account of it, given by Matthew, Mark and Luke, was so solemn and so incontrovertible that the first Christians made it the focal point of their liturgy. When St. Paul reprimanded the Corinthians, who had allowed the "Supper of the Lord" to degenerate into a drunken orgy, he described this meal in the same terms as the synoptics. We repeat these same actions and words at the consecration at Mass today. "This is my Body… This is my Blood." It is simple, precise, divine, and, as the psalm states, "the simple understand."

Baptism and Eucharist — they are tightly interconnected. The Eucharist "actualizes" for us here and now those "things" we were given in baptism. It renews before our eyes that death and resurrection in which we were "buried" at our baptism. It makes sensible, visible, "touchable" (St. John) the presence of the Word of Life. It "feeds" our life in Jesus, purifies it, strengthens it. Through Holy Communion, Jesus "dwells" in us and this same Holy Communion makes visible our union with all the members of the "Body of Christ," with the whole Church. This consecrated Bread and Wine are the pledge, the seed, of our own resurrection. *Anyone who eats my flesh and drinks my blood has eternal life and I shall raise that person up on the last day* (Jn 6:54).

16

"Let it be done according to your Word"

Luke 1:38

We are able to believe in a revealed mystery providing the Father draws us. But we seem to be more ill-at-ease when we have to live that mystery at each instant. The more need we have to touch, see, and feel in order to "realize," that is, in order to concretize any given mystery no matter how ordinary it is, the more that mystery fades into the realm of the mythical. Let us then question those "flesh and bone people," those real beings, those people who have the same human nature as ourselves, who know how to mingle harmoniously in their day-to-day life the things of heaven and earth. Why not begin with Mary of Nazareth?

The reason we take her as our example is because after the birth of Jesus and the exile in Egypt, Mary's daily life was the very epitome of the ordinary, and that is something we should impress upon ourselves. In the eyes of all the good people of Nazareth, she was the wife of Joseph the carpenter, the mother of a son who would become a carpenter — a working man, looked down upon almost as much as a peasant or a slave! She lived like any other woman in Nazareth, taking care of her household chores, going to the market, cooking for her family. One can picture her toting her water jug on her shoulder or balancing it on her head as she went down to draw water from the village well, which incidentally exists even to this day. In their conversations neither she nor Joseph followed up on what had taken place at the Annunciation or the birth of Jesus — that was the secret of the King! Maybe neighbors close to the family, seeing her at prayer or being attentive to the needs of others and showing a willingness to help them, would have suspected something about her and Joseph. But she was simply Mary of Nazareth.

What was it then that transformed this stereotyped existence into holiness beyond all holiness? The answer is found in two words: *Fiat*, meaning yes, and *Jesus*.

Fiat — yes, is the response she gave to the angel sent by God, when he asked her to be the mother of the Christ. And this *yes* she never took back. She is all *yes* without any *no*. Everything she did, said, felt, experienced; all of her sufferings and joys — everything about her was motivated, shot through, by her initial, basic commitment: *yes*. *Yes* to the exile in Egypt; *yes* to the hidden life in Nazareth; *yes* to Jesus' leaving her for his public life; *yes* to the Cross; *yes* to the Resurrection; *yes* to Pentecost. In her, like Jesus, "is found the Yes to all God's promises" (2 Cor 1:20).

Jesus. As if she were not one with him! Her life was completely in step with his. As his mother, she had many opportunities each day to repeat his loving name. Others around her would say it too, but she alone could give it its full meaning. She loaded it with all her "souvenirs": the visit of the angel at the Incarnation, the night of his birth at Bethlehem, the prophecy of Simeon in the Temple, and so many others as well. Everything she heard about him or saw in him "she treasured and pondered in her heart" (Lk 2:19, 51). She lived with Jesus, through Jesus, for Jesus, in Jesus. There was no need for him to be present to her in his physical form; all she had to do was close her eyes to rejoin him in spirit and in truth. He "dwelt" within her.

17

"If we have died to sin, how could we go on living in it?"

Romans 6:2

Perhaps Mary's role in life appears exceptional to us. Was she not, from the very moment of her conception, "full of grace"? She was total *yes* to the Father as no other creature could be. Let us then take a look at other examples, these made up of some ordinary, run-of-the-mill baptized with whom we can identify.

Among those we could pick, there are St. Paul's neophytes, newly converted, baptized pagans. They received the Word from Paul; they possessed "the things of the Kingdom." But they had to live their daily lives, whether they wanted to or not, in a pagan atmosphere, surrounded by those whose mentality and lifestyles were opposed to their own. How could their "attachment to Jesus Christ" not be affected by their surroundings? They did not renege on their baptismal promises; they did not say *no* to Jesus, but they did not give him an unqualified *yes* either. How far could they go in making compromises? Did they themselves know? If one believes the letters of Paul to the Corinthians (1 Cor 4:9-10) and to the Galatians (5:16-21), they sometimes went pretty far indeed. Now what did Paul do to bring them back to "the truth of life"? He certainly did not use psychological therapy on them, nor did he give them moralizing sermons. He vigorously reminded them of the realities they had taken on by their baptismal promises. Their sins excluded them from the Kingdom of God. "You cannot have forgotten that all of us, when we were baptized into Christ Jesus, were baptized into his death" (Rm 6:3). "But now you are set free from sin ('I renounce Satan') and bound to the service of God ('I attach myself to Christ forever'), your gain will be sanctification and the end will be eternal life" (Rm 6:22). Then Paul went on in his customary style to point out to these Christians that if they really lived Christian lives they would show the effects, the "fruit," of this spiritual reality in their everyday lives: "the fruit of the Spirit is love, joy, peace, patience, kindness, goodness, trustfulness, gentleness and self-control" (Gal 5:22). "Since we are living by the Spirit," he added with this beautiful phrase, "let our behavior be guided by the Spirit" (Gal 5:25).

"To bear fruit through sanctity." This is another way of saying to give an unqualified *yes* to Jesus, and through Jesus to the Father. In making this point Paul sums up what makes saints saints. It is remarkable to see how the fathers and doctors in the early Church handed down these most holy mysteries of the faith to the Christian people in such a straightforward manner. Gradually over the course of time, this emphasis gave way to putting a stress on the psychological approach. Preachers of the Gospel spoke of "ways" and "methods" for obtaining holiness; sanctity was walled up, so to speak, in monasteries and cloisters. And the "little children" — what of them? The "poor and lowly" among the ordinary people — what was there for them? Fortunately, there was always a current of teaching that did not keep them out of the mainstream. In Europe names like Erasmus, Gerson, and most especially Francis de Sales were conspicuous in defending this mysticism of the little ones. In his Preface to the *Introduction to the Devout Life*, St. Francis de Sales wrote: "Up until now almost everyone who has treated the subject of devotion has had in mind men and women who have left the world. My intention is to instruct those who live in towns, in families; people who, for all outward appearance, lead ordinary lives, and who frequently will not so much as think of attempting to live a devout life because they imagine that such a life would be impossible for them." He then repeats the gist of St. Paul's words when he concludes: "God asks Christians to produce fruits of devotion, each one according to his ability, state of life, and occupation." Vatican II, especially in chapters four and five of *Lumen Gentium*, gives the fullness of meaning to this type of spirituality.

18

"For though the will to do what is good is in me, the power to do it is not"

Romans 7:18

St. Paul himself admitted that he did not understand his own behavior, "I do not act as I mean to, but I do the things I hate" (Rm 7:18). We are beings torn apart by contradictions, split between what is good and what is evil, and the evil is often the stronger of the two. God says, *The virtuous man falls seven times*, which in biblical terms means often (Pr 24:16).

What power deep within me works against my being faithful to my baptismal promises? It is the sinful "me" to whom Satan promises, just as he promised Adam and Eve, that I will "be like God" if I give in to the covetous desires, pride, and passions he sets before me.

To struggle is not to be unfaithful. It is essential that we realize this during those times of spiritual combat. In fact, the opposite is true. Fighting offers us the opportunity to show that we are sincere in our "attachment to Jesus Christ." As long as we do not freely and deliberately say *yes* to the Tempter, he gains no victory over us, notwithstanding the violence or insidiousness of his assaults. Just as in a siege of a city, there is no victory as long as the citadel, the final point of defense, resists, even though the city and the surrounding suburbs are overcome, so long as we hold out against Satan with St. Paul's defiant challenge: "Can anything cut us off from the love of Christ?" (Rm 8:36), not only are we not vanquished, but we are the victors.

Jesus himself shows us how to be successful in the face of temptation. He was "led by the Spirit out into the desert to be put to the test by the Devil" (Mt 4:1). And that happened right after he was baptized by John the Baptist! He actually let himself be subjected to three terrible assaults. And how did he withstand them? Not by human arguments or psychologizing, but by words from the Bible. Far from denying Satan's power to keep his promises, Jesus hurled him back with the only power that was greater than his, namely by God's Word. When Paul prayed to be delivered from "a thorn in the flesh," the Lord answered him: *My grace is enough for you, for power manifests itself most fully in weakness* (2 Cor 12:9).

It is true that at times Paul gave his Christians who were being tempted advice that contained a more warlike tone. He spoke to them of "breastplates," "helmets," "boots," and "belts" — all of which made up "the armor of God" (Eph 6:13). But then he adds: "Then you must take salvation as your helmet and the sword of the Spirit which is the word of God."

Temptation can enable us to verify the sincerity of our faith, the authenticity of our love of God, the firmness of our hope, and as such, it can be a test that is precious indeed. It certainly lets us see our weakness as creatures and it brings us back to the reality of our human condition. It points to us the "slimy, stinking, fetid" depths we have inherited from our fathers according to the flesh. In short, it introduces us to genuine humility, that virtue that allows God to act freely in us and to shower us with his gifts: "an imperishable, undefiled, and unfading inheritance which is reserved in heaven for you who are being kept safe by God's power through faith until the salvation which has been prepared is revealed at the final point of time" (1 P 1:4-7). And St. Peter goes on to say: "This is a great joy to you, even though for a short time yet you may have to bear all sorts of trials, so that the worth of your faith, more valuable than perishable gold which is tested by fire, may be proved and shown worthy of praise, glory and honor when Jesus Christ is revealed."

19

"This son of mine was dead and has come back to life"

Luke 15:24

We dream a beautiful dream if we think we can go through life without ever falling, and falling gravely. Although occasionally God does give his grace to certain privileged individuals who realize that dream, nevertheless for the rest of us, St. Francis de Sales's wise words ring true: "As we make our way down the road of life, we will always have the need to wash away the dust from our feet." That is to say, we have an ever-present need for the sacrament of reconciliation. So we should not let our failures discourage us. The Lord tells us that *the virtuous man falls seven times*, and then he adds, *although he stands up again*. And that standing up again is what differentiates him from the wicked man (Pr 24:16).

"But I find I keep confessing the same things." "Why should I waste the priest's time?"

"I find it awkward confessing to a man; if I sin I go directly to God."

By saying such things we demonstrate clearly that we consider sacramental confession purely a man-made rite, and consequently we wrongly downgrade the meaning of the sacrament which our faith teaches us is our "immersion in Jesus' death and resurrection." It is a rebirth because in confession we say *no* to Satan and we "attach ourselves forever to Jesus Christ."

Let us therefore take these facts seriously. And to begin with, let us be sincere, frank and honest. Let us not hedge about with our conscience. One cannot be phony with God. Let us admit up front how we wound his heart by our sin.

Honesty? Yes, and not only with our lips but with our hearts as well. Sincerity of heart implies a true desire, a firm will ("a firm purpose") not to fall back into the same sin again. Is a child really sincere when he tells his mother or father that he is sorry for what he has done and, at the same time, is ready to start all over again doing what he said he is sorry for? And let us not be too quick to put the full blame for our actions on temperament (those psychological complexes!), or on society.

Beyond all else, let us believe that our heavenly Father has an infinite desire to forgive us for all that we have done. To despair of his compassionate forgiveness is worse than any sin we could commit. God gives us even more assurance than the father in the parable of the prodigal son, who waited and watched for his son's return, who saw him coming while he was still a long way off, who ran to meet him and who, without even allowing him to say a word, "clasped him in his arms and kissed him." The reasons that prompted the son's return were hardly impressive — hunger, humiliation, destitution. His *pecavi* — "I have sinned" — did not exactly come from a heart befitting a true son. But what difference did that make to the father? He gave the boy festive robes, organized a lavish feast for him with dancing and singing. What a picture of God's mercy! In the sacrament of reconciliation God gives to his contrite and repentant sons all of "those things" that were bestowed upon them in baptism, and which sin took away. And he gives these to them unsparingly.

The older son's reaction in the parable shows us that such mercy goes beyond our comprehension. The older son does not understand! St. Paul also asserts that there is something about God's pardon that goes beyond all human reckoning. He writes: "So it is a proof of God's own love for us, that Christ died for us while we were still sinners" (Rm 5:8).

Felix culpa — "happy fault" was St. Augustine's reaction to Adam's sin. *Felix culpa* is also what we can say about our own sins, providing that, after being pardoned, these sins leave us more humble and more generous. These two virtues, humility and generosity, go together. The love of God is aroused in us whenever we experience our weakness and that, in turn, encourages us to place our confidence in his infinite power rather than in our own resources. St. Francis de Sales teaches that humility without generosity is dangerous, as is generosity without humility. The two go in tandem and together they form solid Christians.

20

"Knowing the love of Christ...
you may attain to the utter fullness
of God himself"

Ephesians 3:19

The more faith we have in the gift of our baptism
the more peace, light, strength, and freedom in-
crease within us to the extent that eventually they
penetrate the very inmost recesses of our being.
We feel overwhelmed by that complete joy which
St. John wanted to share with his Christian flock
(1 Jn 1:4). It is a fullness that comes from the fullness of Christ: "From his fullness we have, all of
us, received" (Jn 1:16). This unanticipated sharing in the fullness of Christ inspired Paul's elo-
quence in his letter to the Ephesians: "This, then,
is what I pray, kneeling before the Father from
whom every fatherhood, in heaven and on earth,
takes its name. In the abundance of his glory may
he grant you inner strength and power through
his Spirit. May Christ dwell in your hearts through
faith, firmly rooted and established in love, so that

with all the saints... you may be filled with the utter fullness of God" (Eph 3:14-19).

What is this fullness? Let us look at the word itself. Fullness means wholeness, plenitude, a filling-up to the total capacity, a diffusive brimming over, and when this meaning is applied to life, it refers to a condition in which the innate desires of our very being are completely satisfied. But God is Love. Therefore if we "are filled with the utter fullness of God," it means that we are filled with Trinitarian love, the love with which the Father, Son, and Holy Spirit love one another; the same love with which they love every creature. St. John tells us: "No one has ever seen God; it is the only Son, who is close to the Father's heart, who has made him known" (Jn 1:18). And so concretely the fullness of God for us is union with Christ "because God wanted all fullness to be found in him" (Col 1:19).

Again we are invited to look to the person of Jesus, God made man, living, resurrected, glorified by the Father. Paul insists on bringing us back to the humanity of Christ: "In him, in bodily form, lives divinity in all its fullness" (Col 2:9). "He is the image of the unseen God, the first born of all creation... and he is the Head of the Body, that is the Church. He is the Beginning, the first-born from the dead... because God wanted all fullness to be found in him and through him to reconcile all things to him by making peace through his death on the cross" (Col 3:15-20). What realism! Jesus is the absolute, unique, sole, efficacious point of passage by which we "attain to the fullness of God himself." The realization of this fact inspired the Apostle to cry out with one of his most penetrating sentences: "There is only one Christ: he is everything and he is in everything" (Col 3:11).

Ever since our baptism this total and totalizing Jesus "dwells" within us; we make but "one with him," as St. Paul tells us; we live his life. How beautiful and true is that "elevation" in the Mass when, as we offer the Father the consecrated bread and wine, we say: "Through him, with him, in him, in the unity of the Holy Spirit, all glory and honor is yours, almighty Father, for ever and ever." Through this liturgical act, which is the Mass, our fullness enters into the fullness of God.

It is the heart that adjusts the vision. The thoughts and feelings of our heart determine the purity and rectitude with which we view people and events. So, if our heart is a "new heart," overflowing with the fullness of Christ, we will see people and the circumstances of life with the same vision as Jesus Christ sees them; that is to say, we will regard them with a vision of love, compassion and hope. Such is the re-birth of vision that comes to the baptized who lives out his baptism.

21

"He explained to them the passages throughout the Scriptures that were about himself"

Luke 24:27

Because "the things of the Kingdom" — God's marvels that we cannot even imagine — can only be known through revelation, the whole of our Christian life depends on the strength of our faith, this faith that we have confessed at our baptism but which must be authenticated during the course of our lives. What is it that nourishes this faith if not an ever deepening knowledge of the books where God himself speaks to us about himself? That is, the Scriptures.

Jesus is the living and eternal center of Scripture. He fulfilled the prophecies written about him before he was born among men, and through his Spirit he is present in all of human history since his Resurrection and Ascension. So it is by looking at Jesus, hearing Jesus, living Jesus, that our faith progresses, develops and is sustained. When we read and re-read Scripture with this thought in mind, particularly the Gospels, we discover the pure, sound, and overflowing fountain of our faith. This is the purpose of *lectio divina*, the "reading of divine things," which should be a commonplace exercise among Christians. It is through this practice that one gradually develops "new eyes."

All of which is an artless way of saying that by simply reading the New Testament we get a sense of realism that we will want to put into practice. The authors of the Gospels, the Acts of the Apostles, the letters of Paul, James, Peter and John are the living witnesses to what they "saw and heard." After Peter and John had cured the paralytic at Jerusalem's Beautiful Gate, the Sanhedrin "threatened them against ever speaking to anyone in [Jesus'] name again." Peter and John retorted, "'You must judge whether in God's eyes it is right to listen to you and not to God. We cannot stop proclaiming what we have seen and heard'" (Ac 4:19-20). "Having seen and heard" and "witnessing with authority" go together. When St. John wanted to communicate his joy to the early Christians, so that their joy "may be complete," he told them, "what we have looked upon and what we have touched with our own hands, the Word of life... we are declaring to you what we have seen and heard" (1 Jn 1:1-3). Before this, there were the shepherds at the birth of Christ. After they had seen "a baby wrapped in swaddling clothes and lying in a manger," they "went back glorifying and praising God for all they had heard and seen" (Lk 2:20). Then, at Christ's transfiguration there was the voice of the Father, *This is my Beloved Son. Listen to him* (Mk 9:7), for the Son knows the Father and the Father communicates his thoughts to the Son.

The apparition of the risen Jesus to the two disciples on the road to Emmaus is a good example for us to see how Jesus reveals himself. At first he walked along with the disciples without giving them any indication of who he was, and they confided in him their sadness and their feelings of having been deceived. Peter and John had already gone off to the tomb running "and had found everything as the women had reported, but of him they saw nothing." Then "he explained to them the passages throughout the Scriptures that were about himself." He kept his identity under the guise of a pilgrim, but when he was with them that evening "at table, he took the bread and said the blessing; then he broke it and handed it to them. And their eyes were opened and they recognized him" (Lk 26:13-35).

Lectio divina is likewise intimately connected with the liturgy. The liturgy of the Eucharist in particular is fundamentally the acting out of *lectio divina*. Reading Scripture also nourishes our faith, renders the living Jesus present in us and disposes us to see that day "when he is revealed, when we will be like him, for we will see him as he is" (1 Jn 3:2).

22

"God saw all he had made, and indeed it was very good"

Genesis 1:31

There are many ways a person can look at creation. The vision of an artist or a painter will not be like that of an astronomer or a biologist. A farmer will not see the world about him in the same way that a hiker or a philosopher will. Everyone sees creation according to who and what he is.

The Christian is no different from others. But the vision of every Christian, irrespective of his background, is mirrored by a different play of light. His eyes are the eyes of the Son of God, and this world is his Father's creature. This was the way Jesus regarded the world and all that is in it during his own lifetime.

The first chapter of the Book of Genesis tells us about the relationship of God with the works of his hand. At each step of creation, God looked at his work, "and he saw that it was good." After the sixth day, God saw all that he had made, "and indeed it was very good." In fact, this work was prodigious. Not only did he create everything he saw ("create" — this is the key-word, the word that is unique in all cosmologies), but he endowed this whole living world with his own creative power, ordering what he had created to multiply, cover all the earth, fill the waters of the seas: *Be fruitful.* And he told man to multiply and *fill the earth and subdue it. Be masters of the fish of the sea, the birds of heaven and all living animals on the earth* (Gn 1:22, 28). The Old Testament contains many a "Hymn to the Universe," wherein wonder turns to adoration, praise and thanksgiving, but there is no more beautiful example of such a hymn than Jesus' words: *Consider the lilies of the field, how they grow; they neither toil nor spin, yet I tell you, even Solomon in all his glory was not clothed like one of these* (Mt 6:28-29). Moreover, the Christian knows full well that the Creator's power goes infinitely beyond anyone's ability to understand. Even though man is ever investigating nature, he accepts the fact that he does not know the secret even of the most commonplace things — the life of an ordinary leaf from a tree, the complexity of a bee's brain, the unfathomable space of the universe. Without understand such things, he accepts their mystery.

The Christian is not a dreamer. He is forced to admit that the creation before which he stands in awe is "deformed." The Bible gives him the reason why — man's desire to become God. Man's lie, his pride have destroyed the divine economy of the first creation. Man has become a "wolf" to man. And in order to commit his crimes, his robbing and plundering, in order to carry on his wars and genocides, he uses that very nature that showers its treasures upon him. Are not all the world's resources — harvests of food, flocks of animals, gold, silver — entrusted to him as a good steward to make the world a place for "all living things on earth"? And the rich man who possesses them makes them the instrument of his tyrannies, ambitions and pleasures. "Will the evil-doers not understand? They eat up my people as though they were eating bread, and they never pray to the Lord" (Ps 14:4). In the Gospel Jesus curses them: *Go away from me into the eternal fire prepared for the Devil and his angels* (Mt 25:41).

But the Christian also knows that, even though creation is held in bondage to sin, there is hope. St. Paul tells him that "the whole of creation is waiting with eagerness for the children of God to be revealed. It was not for its own purposes that creation had frustration imposed on it, but for the purposes of him who imposed it — with the intention that the whole creation itself might be freed from its slavery to corruption and brought into the same glorious freedom as the children of God" (Rm 8:19-20). This liberation will not come about until the end of time, but in the meanwhile, the Christian can "liberate" creation by living each day as a child of God. He can use it, admire it, enjoy it, and delight in it, according to the design of "his Father, the Lord of heaven and earth." Until the new world comes about "Christ is everything and he is in everything" (Col 3:11).

23

"The Tree of the Knowledge of Good and Evil in the middle of the Garden"

Genesis 2:9

We should stress how we deal with the world about us because it influences to a great extent how we relate to God. Take for example the tree. Whether it stands alone or grows in a forest, it is man's companion from cradle to grave, and it is a privileged object that shows us how we regard all created things in relation to the Son of God. Moreover, isn't it a world in itself?

The Bible opens and closes with a vision of paradise, an Eden, where trees are in profusion and where they play a mysterious role. "The Lord God caused to spring up from the soil every kind of tree, enticing to look at and good for food, with the tree of life and the tree of the knowledge of good and evil in the middle of the garden" (Gn 2:9). This is the beginning of our forests, which still cover some twenty-four million square miles or thirty-four per cent of the earth's surface. And the Eden that is described in the Book of Revelation is something even more mysterious: "Then the angel showed me the river of life... Down the middle of the city street, on either bank of the river were the trees of life, which bear twelve crops of fruit in a year, one in each month, and the leaves of which are the cure for the nations" (Rv 22:1-2). So, what is this tree of life of the first paradise and what are these trees of life of the heavenly Jerusalem?

After Adam's fall, God made a decision that helps us to answer these questions: *See, the man has become like one of us, with his knowledge of good and evil. He must not be allowed to stretch out his hand and next pick from the tree of life also, and to eat some [fruit from it] and live forever*, and so God banished him from Eden and "posted cherubim, and the flame of a flashing sword, to guard the way to the tree of life" (Gn 3:22-23). So the tree of life is presented as a source of immortal life for us, life that goes beyond man's mortal nature.

Trees in themselves were not affected more than any other material, living creature by God's curse on Adam. But, along with all the rest of creation, they were subjected by his empty pride, that is to say, by the sin of man. They too groan in labor pains, waiting "with eagerness for the children of God to be revealed." They too hope "to be freed from the slavery of corruption and to be brought into the same glorious freedom as the children of God" (Rm 8:18-22). Let us translate all of this in terms of our daily life. The trees, their flowers, and fruit are for each one of us instruments of salvation or of sin, according to whether we live in accordance with the "empty pride" or the "freedom" of the children of God.

Actually, the tree can be something sacred for man. David and Solomon obtained large quantities of the cedars of Lebanon from King Hiram of Tyre, and had a great deal of lumber brought to Jerusalem to line the Temple walls with paneling in order to close off the Holy of Holies, the altar of perfumes… St. Helen had the first frame structure built over the Holy Sepulcher… But perhaps the tree was also the symbol of power and pride, as at the palace of Herod, or as material for idolatrous practices. Statues of pagan gods were made from wood. These are only two examples; the Bible is full of events, prophecies, dreams, and visions in which God uses the tree as a sign of blessing or curse, as a way to make himself understood by man. And we should mention that there are more than a hundred different types of trees enumerated in Scripture.

We have already spoken of the vine, but let us now focus our attention on three important characteristics of Jesus, the Word made flesh, and see how they are revealed by the image of the tree.

In his wonderful prophecy announcing the coming of the Messiah, Isaiah speaks in this manner: "A shoot shall sprout from the stump of Jesse [the father of David], and from his roots a bud shall blossom. The Spirit of the Lord shall rest upon him" (Is 11:1). And the prophecy continues by describing wonderful world of peace and harmony that the Messiah will inaugurate. Then we read: "On that day, the root of Jesse shall stand as a signal to the peoples. It will be sought out by the nations and its home will be glorious. That day the Lord will raise his hand once more to ransom the remnant of his people (Is 11:10-11).

In no passage is Jesus himself described as the "Tree of Life," but by dying on the wood of the cross, he changed that gibbet of death into the tree that heals and gives life (1 P 2:24).

Thus St. Paul is able to present Christ as "the olive tree itself" on which "the shoots of wild olives [the pagans] have been grafted." And he goes on without paying too much attention to the natural laws governing the grafting process: "Remember that you do not support the root; it is the root that supports you" (Rm 11:16-18).

All along the course of Jesus' life we find trees. There is the manger in the stable of Bethlehem; the carpenter's workshop; the branches from trees, palm fronds, and pieces of greenery that the people cut down to mark his triumphal entry into Jerusalem, and there are the olive trees at Gethsemane. How is it possible for us not to love these life-long companions of ours?

24

"Be strong and show yourself a man"

1 Kings 2:2

The attitude of the baptized person toward others rests on two virtues of his faith: by nature every person is "the image of God"; through grace every person is a member of the Body of Christ. Consequently, everyone has a double claim to brotherhood — according to nature and according to grace. The baptized person would have to be blind indeed not to realize that this fact is dismissed with a laugh in the real world where people deal with each other. Where is the country and when is the time that homicide under all of its forms is unknown? The study of history and the experience of everyday life teaches us that man's world is a jungle.

"Man is a wolf to man," as the Latin proverb has it, but for the Christian the Gospel replies, "Man is a god to man." It would be sanctimonious however not to claim that our instinctive reaction toward "the other" is to fend him off. At the very least, he is an outsider for us, a "foreigner," often an intruder, sometimes a rival or an enemy.

For this reason the baptized has to reach beyond his natural inclinations. The Gospel helps him mightily in giving him reasons for doing so.

Take for example the parable of the Good Samaritan. There was a man on his way from Jerusalem to Jericho who fell into the hands of robbers. They stripped him, beat him, and "left him half dead." A priest, going down the road, saw him, and walked around him. A Levite did the same. Later on, a Samaritan — that is, a "foreigner"! — came along the same road; he bandaged the man's wounds, lifted him onto his own mount, brought him to an inn, and left him in the care of the innkeeper to whom he gave payment in advance. The question Jesus then asked the specialist of the Law casts an uncompromising light on who is my neighbor: *Which of these three, do you think, proved himself a neighbor to the man who fell into the bandits' hands?* The lawyer answered, "The one who showed pity towards him." So, a foreigner, who has not as yet the slightest revelation of "the things of the Kingdom," can practice charity for the simple reason that he is a man.

What light the teachings of Vatican II shed for us on what we term "human wisdom," that is, the wisdom of a non-believer who is sincere in searching for the truth! "The intellectual nature of the human person is perfected by wisdom and needs to be. For wisdom gently attracts the mind of man to a quest and a love for what is true and good. Steeped in wisdom, man passes through visible realities to those which are unseen" (*Gaudium et Spes*, 15).

But even though human pity and human wisdom are beautiful in a sincere non-believer, Jesus demands even more of those in whom he dwells by reason of their baptism. *Love your enemies, do good to those who hate you, bless those who curse you, pray for those who treat you badly… You will be the children of the Most High, for he himself is kind to the ungrateful and the wicked* (Lk 6:27-36). This command is of such a nature that if we do not put it into practice, God will not pardon us. By his pardoning those who nailed him to the cross, Christ gives us an example of how we should live out his new command. Better yet, he had pity on us when he took upon himself our sins so that the justice of his Father would be satisfied.

This new "wisdom" of Jesus obviously revealed what is called "the folly of the cross." *Unless the Father draws him*, one cannot possibly understand, much less practice, such folly. But if the baptized person takes on God's way of seeing, how different will be the meaning of such words as brotherhood, togetherness, compassion, sharing, that we give lip-service to but do not really practice. The Christian can work toward reconciliation in this area, right where he is, with his talents and in the circumstances he finds himself, and he can do so in a totally joyful way. From this reconciliation is born the precious and indispensable gift that the Lord calls "peace." Peace is not only the word associated with the Resurrected Christ, but it is also the word the angels used earlier at Bethlehem. It is peace that the Lord gives us when he meets us along the road we travel (Lk 7:50). This peace is the by-product of his Passion: "But now in Christ Jesus, you who used to be so far off have been brought close, by the blood of Christ. For he is the peace between us" (Eph 2:13-14).

25

"All find their home in you"

Psalm 87:7

The vision that the baptized person has when he looks at the history of the Church can only be one filled with sadness. It is the vision that Jesus had as he wept over Jerusalem and prophesied its ruin: *Jerusalem, Jerusalem. How often have I longed to gather your children together, as a hen gathers her chicks under her wings, and you refused* (Mt 23:37). Wars between Christians, schisms, heresies, not to speak of rivalries that stem from precedence, money — all of this has placed us far from the unity that Christ said would be the sign by which all would recognize that we were his disciples. Let us honestly admit it: the robe of the visible Church is sullied by the sins of men, even sometimes by those who hold the most exalted and sacred positions in the Church.

All of this is known and recognized to be the factual truth. But at the same time, the fair thing to do is to draw up a balance sheet and to show what the Church has meant and what it continues to mean to Christians.

— In spite of its faults and the sins of its members and ministers, it has been, and remains, the sacramental source of divine life. It does so through the sacraments of Baptism, Penance, and the Holy Eucharist. The Christian whom God has called to the ministerial priesthood has the certainty that his ordination binds him by an uninterrupted chain to the apostles. The Church is apostolic, doctrinally and liturgically.

— In spite of internal divisions, the Church is the center of my unity with my baptized brothers and sisters and with all men and women of goodwill, the place where all "searchers for God" are welcomed. Its documents are carefully and studiously read, even by non-believers. Free to be criticized and rejected, the Church's teachings leave no one indifferent.

— Even in the darkest hours of her history, the Church has remained faithful to her mission: *Go, make disciples of all nations: baptize them in the name of the Father and of the Son and of the Holy Spirit.* She prolongs in time and space the work of Jesus Christ.

— Through her saints and martyrs, men and women, canonized or known to God alone, she keeps alive in a world that is constantly reverting to paganism the presence and the word of our Savior Jesus Christ. And in doing so, she gives meaning to our common destiny. The Church is holy.

— Irrespective of who they are, the Church gives devoted and generous care to the sick, to those who hunger more for love than for food, to the abandoned, the homeless and marginal, and to all the rejects of our society. In the eyes of those men and women who see Christ himself in the suffering and the poor, the poorer they are the better, and the more conscientiously and tenderly they are served.

— In the midst of a swirling, fast-moving world of shattered nerves and dreams, of exploited fads, vanities, violence and sex, the Church prays. She raises up to God the praise and thanksgiving that are due to him as Creator and Savior of all. For the millions of priests and religious this prayer is the *opus divinum*, the divine work *par excellence*. It is their "mission."

Such is the Church, and because she is who she is we can honestly sing the psalm of Zion: "Philistia, Tyre, Ethiopia, these will be her children, but Zion shall be called 'Mother' for all shall be her children. It is he, the Lord Most High, who gives each his place. In his register of peoples he writes: 'These are her children,' and while they dance they will sing: 'In you all find their home'" (Ps 87). The reason why the Church is such a prolific mother is because she is the "Body of Christ." Her "breath of life" comes from the Spirit of the Father and Son. Just as the Spirit goes about doing his work from age to age, his work of salvation, so he works to bring about unity, holiness and love in the Church that is all too human in so many ways.

We should not forget that each one of us is the Church, and that every day, wherever we are, we should go about with Christ in building up the Church. But this "vocation" of ours should not crush us because "as a child has rest in its mother's arms, even so my soul," as we read in Psalm 131. Our mother the Church is worthy of our love.

26

"Say: Our Father…"

Matthew 6:9

In this prayer that Jesus himself taught his disciples we have all "the things of the Kingdom" that we have meditated on. But only those who are "attached to Jesus Christ" are able to give it its full meaning. When the seventy-two disciples returned from their mission, Jesus said a prayer that sprang from his heart and in it he repeated three times the word "Father." *I bless you, Father, Lord of heaven and earth for hiding these things from the learned and the clever and revealing them to little children. Yes, Father, for that is what it pleased you to do.* Then there was the "Our Father." An ancient writer recommended that the common people who could not read should mark off their days with the "Our Father." He called this prayer "the breviary of the poor."

Exegetes tell us that the word *Abba* (Father) was the familiar term Jewish children used for "father," but certainly not for God! So, it is really bold to address God as Father (*Abba*). Whether that is so or not, it is only by the Holy Spirit that we can call God "Father," and we do because we are his sons. "The proof that you are sons is the fact that God has sent forth into our hearts the Spirit of his Son which cries out *Abba*, Father" (Gal 4:6).

According to St. Luke, it was after the disciples had seen Jesus at prayer that they asked him, "Lord, teach us how to pray…" And he responded, *When you pray, say…* Was this not a kind of summary of his own prayer put into a few sentences for our benefit, an abridgment of those extended conversations that he, faithful Son that he was, had with the Father? However short, these few sentences would now take on the fullness of God himself. And this is the way that we should understand them because the Our Father brings together all the subjects and all the desires that dwelt in the Heart of Christ during his earthly mission. These are the words that provoked his vision of God and man and that inspired the actions he performed and the words he spoke.

The first two words alone, "Our Father," set the tone and create the atmosphere for the rest of the prayer. They call to mind the new world that Jesus came to establish (or reestablish), where man, should he wish to do so, can begin anew to restore a love-relationship with his Creator and with his brothers and sisters, that is, with every human being throughout the world. The "Our Father" makes sense only when it surges forth from a heart that is both filial and fraternal.

The word "Father" changes the wishes and requests that follow. The Kingdom that one hopes will come about is a Kingdom of love. The divine will that one prays will be done is not the will of a master over his slaves, but the will of the infinite goodness of the omnipotent, omniscient God. The "daily bread" is what children expect to receive for the least of their needs from an attentive hand. The pardon is that which the father showed to the prodigal son, but in order to give it to us, the Father, who is the Father of all men and women, asks that we also pardon one another. Happy indeed is the person who lives such a prayer, for in doing so he lives here on earth in "the freedom and glory of the children of God."

We should not be surprised that the fathers of the Church and great mystics were so taken with making commentaries on the "Our Father." At the highest point on the Mount of Olives in Jerusalem there is a Carmelite monastery where the words of the "Our Father," written in all the languages of the world, are engraved on the walls of its cloister. What a wonderful vision of the world this scene presents! In a similar manner the Holy Spirit, using the letters of life, engraves on our hearts, at the center of our thoughts, desires and actions, the "Lord's Prayer."

After the consecration at Mass, the congregation says or sings the "Our Father." Is not this the highest moment of our prayer, repeating "Our Father" together with Jesus there present, as bread on our table, the living pardon of our Father "who is in heaven"?

27

"They will still bear fruit when
they are old"

Psalm 92:15

Growing old is something we all have to do. It is a normal process for every living organism on this earth. Like a tree and a bird, a man is born, grows, withers, and dies. And there are as many ways of growing old as there are old people. He who believes in "the things of the Kingdom" and is baptized is, without any doubt, a privileged individual. For such a one, the road goes in the opposite direction: it is less important that he leave an earthly life wrought with danger than that he embark on a new, a more energized life in the world beyond, a life filled with more than anyone can desire, much less imagine. His life here on earth is transfigured by his faith. "So we do not lose heart for even though this outer human nature of ours may be falling into decay, at the same time our inner human nature is renewed day by day" (2 Cor 4:16). This "inner human nature" is being recreated in us in Christ. Already in the "Biblical Canticle" the just are described as "those who are planted in the house of the Lord," and we are told that "they will flourish in the courts of our God, still bearing fruit when they are old, still full of sap, still green, to proclaim that the Lord is just" (Ps 92:14-15).

What are the elements that make the aging process unique for a Christian?

Like every other aging person, the Christian experiences decline in his physical, moral and intellectual vigor. But he strives courageously to draw what is best from the vitality that is still his. Seeing that this remnant of strength is given to him by his heavenly Father, he recognizes it as a "talent" that he should make sure is productive and does not waste away. This attitude leads to his living in a state of continuous gratitude and even adoration.

The aging person carries the past back in memory. No doubt there are dark spots, pictures of infidelities to baptismal promises, but he realizes that God "has thrust all these sins behind his back" (Is 38:17), and that he is pardoned. Simultaneous with these sentiments of thanksgiving and humility is the realization of God's pardon, and this in turn gives rise to enraptured feelings of total abandonment to the mercy of his heavenly Father. Apart from what he reads in the Bible, the old person becomes aware of a vague yet clear, unsettling realization of his basic unworthiness, of the fact that he is a sinner, and therefore he has a need to find refuge in Someone whose compassion is infinite.

"Just as he dies alone, so each one lives alone; others do nothing to change that." This observation of Maurice Blondel is more true for the old person than it is for anyone else. Whether he wants them or not, silence and solitude become his companions making him ever more a hermit. But this loneliness can also awaken in him a line of thought that is truly beneficial. It grounds him in the truth of the human condition wherein he discovers that life is as much a mystery as is light. He comes to see that, despite his efforts "always to be more," he has, in fact, been more dominated by life than he has charted it out for himself. Such meditation opens to an Other, whose "heart is much larger than his own."

Old age for the Christian is certainly the time *par excellence* for prayer. "Lord," said St. Augustine, "you have created us for yourself and our hearts are restless until they rest in you" (*Confessions*, 1:1). The Christian who is aging can understand and relish that repose, that peace that transcends suffering. Christ's words strike him at the heart of his anguish: *Indeed just as the Father raises the dead and gives them life, so also the Son gives life to whomever he wishes* (Jn 5:21). *I have come so that they may have life and have it to the full* (Jn 10:10). Indeed, the aging person has life, but he knows well that he has received it from the life-giving vine planted by the Father among men, and he realizes that "always green and full of sap," he can help his fellow men become alive from the same sap. Vatican II teaches us in such a wonderful way that contemplatives (and who is more contemplative than an old person!) "have a distinctive part to play in Christ's Mystical Body... by imparting a hidden, apostolic fruitfulness, they make [God's] people grow" (*Perfectae Caritatis*, 7). Solitary, they become envoys of solidarity!

Clearly the old person's temperament, history, grace, and environment are contingent factors contributing to the religious perspectives described above. In short, the more his faith, the clearer his vision.

28

"O Death, where is your victory?"

1 Corinthians 15:55

"The wages of sin is death," Saint Paul said, "but the free gift of God is eternal life in Christ Jesus our Lord" (Rm 6:23). We have had this eternal life within us ever since our baptism. "So anyone who is in Christ is a new creation: the old has passed away and behold the new has come!" (2 Cor 5:17). As long as we are here on earth, we get only a glance at this new being, a glimpse through the shadow of faith. After we die we shall see that reality clearly and we shall know it perfectly: "Now I know only in part; then I will know fully, even as I have been fully known" (1 Cor 13:12). "My dear friends, we are already God's children, but what we shall be in the future has not yet been revealed. We are aware that when he appears we shall be like him, because we shall see him as he really is" (1 Jn 3:2). Heaven is God possessed; it is God loved in an eternal instant. Better, it is God possessing us, loving us, uniting himself to us for all eternity. The fundamental, existential desire we have for life, joy, love, and unity will at last be fully satisfied, perfectly gratified. Our hearts will know repose, peace.

St. Paul says that this passage from earthly to eternal life takes place in the twinkling of an eye (1 Cor 15:52). We should relish in full-flavored hope these words from the First Preface of the Mass for the Dead: "Lord, for your faithful people life is changed, not ended." We get some idea, however imperfect, of this wonderful metamorphosis from the grain that dies to give birth to the ear of wheat or the chrysalis that enfolds the butterfly. In the light of this, how terrible was God's punishment after Adam's sin: "You are surely doomed to die" (Gn 2:17).

It is wonderful that there are preludes to this final metamorphosis in our daily lives. Our trials, sufferings, mortifications have repercussions in life eternal: "The temporary, light burden of our hardships is earning for us an eternal fullness of glory which is beyond all comparison" (2 Cor 4:17).

Our faith in Christ's Resurrection is the basis for our faith in this marvelous transformation. St. Paul's argument against those who were teaching the false doctrine that there is no resurrection of the dead is incisive: "If the dead are not raised, neither is Christ; and if Christ has not been raised, our teaching is void of content and your faith is empty too." Then he adds this staggering statement: "If our hope in Christ has been for this life only, we are of all people the most pitiable" (1 Cor 15:13-19). Granted that this conclusion is excessive because Paul himself teaches us that when we imitate Christ in this life we "honor the man," but in the citations above he is underlining the importance in his teaching of Christ's Resurrection.

When the apostles went out to preach after Pentecost, they spoke of nothing else. They built the solid and basic core of their teaching, and consequently of our faith, around the fact that Jesus was born, died, and rose from the dead. This was the central point of their message and they would leave the Church a basic credo that is nothing more than an affirmation of this same doctrine.

Why look for more than what is contained in the simple formula Jesus gave at the time of his Ascension: *Go, therefore, make disciples of all nations; baptize them in the name of the Father and of the Son and of the Holy Spirit* (Mt 28:19)?

"I am resurrected with Christ." We must convince ourselves of this reality, place it at the heart of our daily life, our work, our relations with all of those with whom we come in contact. It must determine our vision of the world because heaven begins here on earth! The Kingdom of Heaven is within us, right now.

29

"He loved me and gave himself for me"

Galatians 2:20

Paul's cry of desperate love has turned many lives topsy-turvy and has brought about numerous conversions. "He loved me." Jesus? Me? Then why do I not know him? Why at times do I refuse that love? Indeed, the nature of Love Eternal is to love. But what is most astounding is that Jesus invites me to love him in return. What can my poor love mean? Whatever… The fact is this: the Christian vocation is an invitation to be loved by Jesus and to love him in return. It is up to me — to my freedom and my will — to respond to that invitation, to say 'yes' or 'no'.

It means to give that response today, as I am now. As a creature, I have my limitations and I am a sinner, but I realize that each person is unique. Following up on what Pliny observed, St. Francis de Sales said: "No two pearls are exactly the same: every one is distinctive; each has its own qualities." Everyone of us is novel as well; each one has his own race, nationality, temperament, family background, friends, areas of interest, a personal record of graces accepted and graces refused. In short, each of us has his own history. Is that history good? Mediocre? A little bit of both, maybe? What difference does it make? The important thing is to be who we are, without pretensions, sham, or phoniness. After all, were Peter, John, Thomas, and other apostles all alike when they responded to Jesus' invitation to "Follow me"? And what about Martha and her sister Mary, and Mary Magdalen — were they all just alike? "Be who you are, but be good — with all your heart and all your might," is what St. Francis de Sales used to tell his many Philotheas, those pious ladies who strove to love God. Love is always fresh and unique, even when it is declared in the same words and by the same actions.

The personalization of our response to Jesus' invitation has many practical consequences on our life of union with God, and in particular on our prayer. Let us pay heed to the advice, methods and "ways" of prayer that people or books suggest, but at the same time remember that true prayer is the prayer that springs forth from our own lives, now, at this moment. Let us be sensitive to those passages that attract our attention as we read our Bible, and particularly let us be responsive to the Scripture readings at Mass. Finally, let us be consciously aware of all those things that go to make our lives humdrum. God speaks to us through all of the motions of our soul and through them he points the way that he wants us to travel. Let "the religion of the present moment" be ours. The past is gone; the future is not yet here. Only the present is real and so, under the uninterrupted inspiration of the Holy Spirit dwelling within us, let us fill each present moment with eternity, with divine life.

In putting this "personal religion" into practice, is there a danger of sealing ourselves off and cutting our neighbor out of our lives? Absolutely not. Just the opposite is so. Our ability to give to others and to be receptive to them is in direct ratio to how much Jesus "lives" in us, dwells within us, to what extent his Spirit moves us. "For the love of Christ urges us on" (2 Cor 5:14). The Holy Spirit tells us at every moment the response we should have, the word we should say (or should not say) in order that "the peace of Christ" reign between us and our neighbor. There is not merely continuity, there is identity between Christ's First and Second Commandment. When the Pharisee cunningly asked Jesus which was the greatest commandment of the Law, Jesus replied: *The second is like the first* (Mt 22:39). Just as in a human body the health of each member has an effect on the soundness of every other part, so it is in the Mystical Body. We influence one another.

This law of life is absolutely essential for the

well-being of families, groups, associations, religious communities, and for all that is deemed "institutional"; consequently, it is indispensable for the visible Church. The well-being, spirit, and effectiveness of every such group depends on the spiritual health of each of its members. Without saying anything noteworthy or doing anything special, a Christian can "metamorphose" his environment merely by living out simply and silently the life he received at baptism. And often that is the only thing he can do for those who make up his community.

30

"Lord, to whom should we go?
You have the words of eternal life"

John 6:68

What other passage of the Gospel could better sum up what is meant by the mysticism of the little ones than these words of Peter? He said everything that there is to say. He asserted that attachment to Jesus, faith in Jesus, is not the conclusion to a reasoning process, nor a miracle, not even one like the multiplication of loaves, but that it is the feeling that those "things" that Jesus revealed satisfy the heart's deepest desires, the desire to live, the desire for life without end. No, no one ever spoke like Jesus, with such authority, such certitude. He spoke about what he knew from experience. Could one expect to hear truer words from any other teacher? "To whom else should we go?" Jesus' "words" were not, nor would they ever be anything more than promises that would say something about the future. *We shall come to him and make a home in him* (Jn 14:23). *Then you will know*

that I am in my Father and you in me and I in you
(Jn 14:20). Now Jesus' Passion-Resurrection-Ascension has "accomplished" these promises; he made them living realities, the "truths of life." Certainly there is an element of mystery in them that remains. But Jesus is the Eternal Word, the Word by which everything came into being. Therefore these words are not merely human words. They are the words of God; they are creative words. "And God said... and all that he said came into being." When we believe in the word of Jesus we have that same assurance, and that assurance is that eternal life is a reality for us. At Capernaum Jesus taught his disciples: *The words I have spoken to you are spirit and they are life* (Jn 6:63).

If you only knew the gift God is offering and who it is who is saying to you, "Give me something to drink..." (Jn 4:10) were the words Jesus spoke to the Samaritan woman. God offers us the gift of himself. Through our faith and baptism, he shares his very life with us. This is indeed something that slakes our thirst; the water that he gives us is for us *a spring of water, welling up for eternal life* (Jn 4:10). This water purifies us to the very depths of our being; it makes us "to be more," always more, it quenches the primordial thirst of our nature by overflowing the capacities of our desires. It leads us to that "river of life, rising from the throne of God and the Lamb, and flowing crystal-clear" that is spoken about in the Book of Revelation (Rv

22:1). Joy, abundance, repose, the fullness of life — this is what is given the baptized who believes in Christ and in his words.

One of the most moderate, yet profound masters of the spiritual life in our times says, "From the very beginning of their spiritual life men and women must catch a glimpse of these realities." We further add that the children placed in our care should, as far as they are able, be made aware and live these realities. In one of his *Pensées* (143), Pascal criticizes those who instruct children from their infancy "with the care" of honor, fortune, the future, and with "diversions," and he says: "We should only have to relieve children from all these cares; then they would see themselves; they would reflect on what they are, whence they came, whither they go…" In other words, they would find "true happiness" in knowing that they are brothers and sisters of Jesus Christ, sons and daughters of God, that they have come from God and that they are going to God. With such an insight, they would be able to put into perspective the concerns they have for their honor, fortune, future and "diversions."

At the beginning of his first letter, St. John "declares eternal life" to "you, my children," and he does so in this instance "so that our joy may be complete" (1 Jn 1:4). "Joy" is the preferred word of the Resurrected Jesus!

A KIND OF EPILOGUE

"Amen! Come Lord Jesus!"

Revelation 22:20

How does one go about gathering together so many heavenly riches in order to display them on a single tableau or say everything about them in one symbol? St. John has attempted the impossible in the Apocalypse or Book of Revelation, particularly in the last two chapters, and, to the extent that he has conjured up and made us feel this unspeakable reality, which is impossible to describe graphically, he has succeeded. He thought of the most precious, the most beautiful, and the most savory things imaginable and then, using them to express his thoughts, he attempted to describe the wonders awaiting all who, from his day to the end of time, will have ever known and served Christ. Let us then have simple hearts like the hearts of little children so that we may briefly experience for ourselves the Apostle's enthusiasm.

First of all, St. John advises us that in this Paradise of eternity everything is completely new.

"I saw a new heaven and a new earth; the first heaven and the first earth had passed away" (Rv 21:1). Absolutely new. Youthful beyond measure. God does not repair the old world; he creates a new one that will last "from eternity to eternity."

And here is the description of the new Jerusalem: "I saw the holy city, the new Jerusalem, coming down out of heaven from God, prepared as a bride dressed for her husband" (Rv 21:2). It is a festive time in the city, preparations are made for the feast *par excellence*. Joy will reign for the "marriage feast of the Lamb" (Rv 21-22). Who is this Lamb? It is he alone who was capable of opening "the scroll that was written on the back and front and was sealed with seven seals" (Rv 5:1), the alpha and the omega of all creation, the "shoot of David." And this Lamb appeared "sacrificed, and with your blood you bought the people of God of every race, language, people and nation" (Rv 5:9). It is Jesus! In presenting him as the sacrificed Lamb, John reminded his readers of the Passover lamb, the memorial meal of Israel's deliverance, and also the Last Supper, the Passover of the Lord, as well as all the Lord's acts of mercy for his people.

The wedding of the Lamb also takes place in the setting of a feast. Singing breaks out from all corners, and what choirs there are, "all the living things in creation — everything that lives in heaven, and on earth, and under the earth, and the sea," and all were loudly singing a new canticle, "and there were ten thousand times ten thousand of them and thousands upon thousands." Their song was directed to "the One seated on the throne and to the Lamb," to whom they sang "all praise, honor, glory and power for ever and ever" (Rv 5:12-13). All of this jubilation was accompanied by harps and lyres.

This feast of beauty and joy was also a feast of light. This was a light that knew not the night. It was eternal. "The city did not need the sun or the moon for light… since it was lit by the radiant glory of God, and the Lamb was a lighted torch for it… There is no night there." All is transparent. Moreover, no one or "nothing unclean may come" into the Temple of Light, "no one who is loathsome or false, but only those who are listed in the Lamb's book of life" (Rv 21:23-27).

John heard a voice coming from this celestial Jerusalem proclaiming from the throne: "'Look, here God dwells among human beings. He will make his home among them; they will be his people, and he will be their God, God-with-them. He will wipe away all tears from their eyes; there will be no more death, and no more mourning or sadness or pain. The world of the past has gone'" (Rv 21:3-4). "To live with; dwell among" is the term John uses in his Gospel to make us understand the indescribable "indwelling" of God in us and we in God.

In the final lines of the Book of Revelation,

Jesus countersigns, so to speak, the apocalyptic revelations of John. *I Jesus…* At that time "the Spirit and the Bride say, 'Come!'… Then let all who are thirsty come; all who desire it may have the water of life, and have it free" (Rv 22:17).

In the face of the wonders wrought by God, who would not be "the one who is thirsty," or "the one who desires"? So, let us draw near and with the Spirit and the Bride, say: "Amen! Come Lord Jesus!"